Over Homestake Pass on ...

The
Butte
Short Line:

The Construction Era 1888-1929

by

Bill & Jan Taylor

Pictorial Histories Publishing Co., Inc.   Missoula, Montana   59801

LIBRARY OF CONGRESS
CATALOG CARD NUMBER 98-65009

ISBN 1-57510-040-1

First Printing March, 1998

*Typography, layout, and
cover by the authors on
Macintosh utilizing:
Aldus Pagemaker 5.0
Adobe Photoshop 3.0
Aldus Freehand 5.1*

PICTORIAL HISTORIES PUBLISHING COMPANY, INC.
713 South Third West, Missoula, Montana 59801

For some rail enthusiasts, collecting places is as natural as collecting things. We find visiting the historical places, especially those of railroad history, as rewarding as adding a piece to our collection at home. Tracking down names on the Northern Pacific timetables has been an outgrowth of being raised in Montana and having an interest in thriving places which have long since become ghost towns. That is what led us east from Butte, Montana, along the Northern Pacific tracks to Welch.

The abandoned granite quarry at Welch is spectacular. Sitting atop the Boulder batholith, just over the continental divide from Butte, its exposed layers alternate with stands of aspen and fir. Ties still line the creek bed where quarry men diverted the water long enough for the trains to reach the upper loading platform. Among the granite remains of power plant and shop buildings linger clues to the people who used to live and work there: shards of purple glass, lengths of chain and cable, even tinware with "NPRR" markings. For us it presents the ideal combination of breathtaking scenery, abandoned mining camp, and Montana history as it was defined by the railroads.

On the Butte side of the divide, the batholith takes the form of mineralized outcroppings. The first practical discovery of gold in 1864 encouraged placer operations, but miners soon began to work deeper. Seasonal water flows limited operations, and besides the mineral veins which seamed the hills on all sides invited exploration. Early copper and silver discoveries languished as attempts to reduce the ore were fruitless. A decade later, however, a new discovery in the Travona lode sent rich silver ore to the smelters at Salt Lake, attracting the attention of miners and capitalists there. Soon Butte had a host of silver mines and mills. Production was strong into the 1890's when declining prices contributed to their closure.

Even as the silver veins were playing out, copper production was on the rise. The Colorado Smelting Company was erected in 1879-80, and its production of copper matte established the industry on a permanent basis. The first railroad reached the district in 1881 with the citizens of Butte bearing the expense of building the last link. While the ex-tensive placer district to the north initially helped convince surveyors to locate the Northern Pacific main line through Helena, Butte would not be over-looked. Eight years later the NP constructed its Gallatin-Butte branch.

Proud of its hard work and accomplishments, Butte set out to fashion itself into a city. The same geology which provided the minerals also provided the building materials. By the turn of the century James Welch's granite quarry along the new Northern Pacific line was producing the foundation stones for Butte's deepest and heaviest buildings. Welch granite, in the form of loaf-sized pavers, smoothed the streets and defined the curbs. When a memorial was raised to mining magnate Marcus Daly in 1906, Welch granite formed the base and the enclosure.

It is our good fortune not only to be able to visit Welch and picnic on dressed stones which missed transport on the last train, but also to read about the exciting times in copies of the *Butte Daily Miner*, *Helena Independent*, *Anaconda Standard*, Whitehall's *Jefferson Valley Zephyr* and other publications of the day which exist in many locations throughout the state. Newspapermen reported on the corporation and individual alike, rounding out our view of both. Through these accounts, we have learned not only of the local efforts to secure a second Northern Pacific line for Butte, but also of the celebration at its completion and the grand excursion to Bozeman over the new line. Corporate records rescued for the state by University of Montana professor K. Ross Toole include the 1889-90 personal correspondence of construction engineer Patterson, right down to his justification for money spent on sandwiches, cigars and liquor on that same Bozeman excursion. Finally, Montana collectors have saved photos, train orders, even hardware from those earliest times to complete the picture.

What began as a day trip to Welch has grown into this book. It has incorporated our separate interests in railroads and old-time newspapers into a research project we would like to share. It is an account of mining, construction, immigration, politics, and railroading--the stuff from which Montana was made.

Jan & Bill Taylor

Acknowledgments

No project of this size could be done by just two people. Many friends and acquaintances who share a common interest in the Northern Pacific Railroad and Montana history have had a hand in this book in countless ways. Unfortunately, they are just too numerous to mention individually.

We must single out a few for special attention, however, because their aid and assistance have been especially helpful. First, we would like to thank Roy Milligan of Whitehall for his generosity in sharing the photo collection of the Jefferson Valley Museum in that city and for allowing us to use the work he did concerning the history of the Jefferson Valley.

Second, a special word of thanks needs to be given Dale Johnson, the recently retired archivist at the University of Montana. Dale directed us to historical NP papers, many of which are in the book. In addition he shared his doctoral thesis concerning A.B. Hammond which contained many pieces of valuable information.

Third, R. Milton Clark of Missoula allowed us to use his research on the dates NP lines were completed in Montana, many of his computer graphics, helped us edit the final text, and advised us on technical matters.

Fourth, we thank Lorenz P. Schrenk of Minneapolis who provided AFE information on Welch Quarry, supplied ICC reports and shared his unpublished manuscript on the Montana Union.

Finally, we need to recognize Warren R. McGee of Livingston who kept us anchored in reality concerning operations on the mountain, shared with us many of his photographs, and served as a cheerleader and sounding board throughout the project.

Thanks to all of you.

The Authors

Bill and Jan Taylor live in Missoula, Montana. Bill teaches English at Big Sky High School, and Jan is a former German teacher and coach. Both are Montana natives who have had a lifelong interest in Montana history. This interest has manifested itself in visiting and photographing many of the ghost towns in the state and researching the rail history. Visiting historical places is their passion. Bill has written a number of magazine articles for historical publications. Jan has turned her attention to historical research and has spoken to numerous genealogical groups concerning railroad names and occupations in the state. This is their first book.

Photo Credit Sources

JE	- John Eberle	WRM	- Warren R. McGee
JVM	- Jefferson Valley Museum	WMM	- World Museum of Mining Collection
JM	- Jim Motzko Collection		
MHS	- Haynes Foundation Collection Montana Historical Society		- All uncredited photos have been taken by the authors or belong to their collection
PHP	- Pictorial Histories Publishing Company Collection		

Table of Contents

*This book is dedicated to the quarrymen
of Welch and their families*

Northern Pacific Railway
1900 *Wonderland*

1. Bound For Butte

PHP

Utah & Northern narrow gauge engine #285 *The Logan* with engineer Charles Hawkins whistles at the Garrison depot in 1884. The freight train will soon head south towards Butte. The depot in the background is the Northern Pacific depot. The NP reached Garrison in 1883.

Butte

Butte, Montana, is located in a mile-high valley along the continental divide in the southwestern part of the state. It remains the center of one of the richest mining districts in the world. Gold was first discovered there in 1864, but further exploration revealed extensive deposits of silver. By 1885 copper had become the most valuable ore.

After the 1869 completion of the first transcontinental railroad which passed through Utah, Butte miners began shipments of ore via a 400 mile wagon road over Monida Pass to Corinne, the nearest station. It was not long before railroad entrepreneurs undertook to build a railroad north over this same route to tap Butte's markets. Their plans took on a more concrete nature when they learned construction of the Northern Pacific had become stalled in the Dakotas as a result its corporate bankruptcy and the financial panic of 1873.

The Utah & Northern

The Utah Northern, a narrow gauge railroad, was built north from Brigham City, Utah, funded initally by private capitalists. Construction reached the Montana border at Monida in 1880 by which time it had become a Union Pacific subsidiary and renamed the Utah & Northern. Construction was completed into Butte via the Big Hole River and Silver Bow on December 21, 1881, making it the first railroad with outside connections to enter the Montana Territory.

The U&N also planned lines to Helena which at that time was the territorial capital and the center of a rich placer gold mining region. Surveys were completed from Dillon along the Jefferson and Missouri Rivers. In an agreement reached with the NP in January, 1882, however, the UP agreed not to extend the U&N to Helena, and the newly resurgent NP agreed not to build through Butte. Narrow gauge tracks were completed by the U&N 40 miles north from Silver Bow to Garrison which was named for William Lloyd Garrison, Henry Villard's father-in-law. This would become the end of the line for the U&N.

The Northern Pacific

By 1881 the resolution of Indian hostilities in eastern Montana and the reorganization of its corporate structure made it possible for the Northern Pacific to begin building again. Construction gangs built east from Washington and west from North Dakota under the energetic leadership of Henry Villard.

Routes had been surveyed by the NP through Butte, but the decision was made to build over the continental divide at Mullan Pass west of Helena instead. It was a route 40 miles shorter and crossed the divide at a point lower than passes east of Butte. The NP's 1882 agreement with the UP, and the accompaning $500,000 payment, solidified the choice of route.

The NP's decision was quite unpopular with the citizens of Butte, and a lobbying campaign began almost immediately to lure it into the Silver Bow Valley. In 1881 one NP civil engineer was fired when he wrote supporting the Pipestone route (later followed by the Milwaukee Road) over the Mullan Pass route put forward by NP's Chief Engineer Adna Anderson, who was in charge of the construction through Montana. He and other NP insiders had invest-

A menu from Villard's opening celebration in Minneapolis, September 5, 1883.

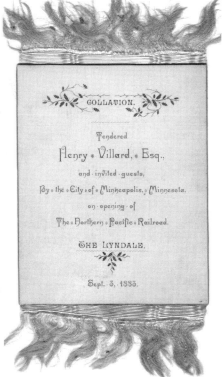

ed in Helena property which further committed them to that route. In 1888 Butte merchants went so far as to commission the Ray railroad survey over Pipestone Pass and give it to the NP.

The NP tracks joined just west of Garrison on September 8, 1883. Ironically, the line up the Jocko Valley, over Evaro Hill and to Gold Creek was built by the same Mormon construction crews originally hired by the U&N to build the roadbed to Helena.

The crossing of Mullan Pass west of Helena was done by a switch back line over the summit until the 3,898' long tunnel was completed (delayed for several weeks because of unstable rock). A few months later Villard's financial empire collapsed, and control of the NP passed into other hands.

In November the Mullan Pass line was officially accepted by Congress and bonds were sold on it

---

This view of Garrison looking to the southeast dates to the summer of 1908. The NP was in the process of rebuilding its main line that year. The new yard and depot are center right. The old Garrison depot and interchange are at center left. This was also the site of the U&N/MU facilities. Across the river is the construction for the new Milwaukee line. Evidence of the summer's flooding can be seen although most of the standing water results from a river channel change done by the railroad. The 1908 rebuild double tracked the line from Garrison to Missoula.

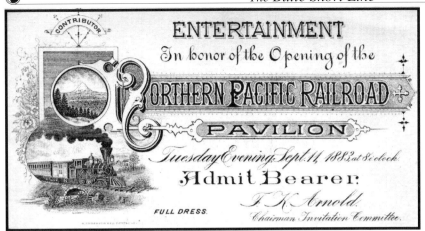

ENTERTAINMENT
In honor of the Opening of the
NORTHERN PACIFIC RAILROAD
PAVILION
Tuesday Evening, Sept. 11, 1883, at 8 o'clock.
Admit Bearer:
F. K. Arnold.
FULL DRESS.
Chairman Invitation Committee.

to provide operating capital for the Northern Pacific. Butte's NP Agent James McCaig, who remained a strong influence throughout this period, explained this to the citizens of Butte who were still voicing a desire for the main line to be moved to the Pipestone route. In a May 2, 1888, interview in the *Butte Semi-Weekly Miner* he said,

The main line via Mullan can never be abandoned on account of the fact that it was accepted by President Arthur as the main thoroughfare to tide-water on Puget Sound. Under the terms of its charter from the Government, the Northern Pacific has, under certain restrictions, been permitted to bond the line at a certain sum per mile. The permanent roadway leading from Helena to Elliston was favorably reported on by Government Commissioners in September, 1883, and the company was then placed in position to issue bonds on that section of the road at the minimum prescribed by Congress.

For the time being, Butte would have to content itself with branch line service from the U&N. Commodities and passengers for the NP would be moved from narrow gauge equipment to standard gauge equipment at Garrison resulting in serious delays, or they would be sent 150 miles over a narrow gauge line to Pocatello.

The Montana Central

Enter James J. Hill. Hill, an ambitious St. Paul railroad magnate, was also looking west from Minnesota in the 1880's. He recognized that for his St. Paul, Minneapolis & Manitoba road (later the Great Northern) to be successful, he needed an extension to Puget Sound. The importance of Butte did not escape him. Hill became a friend of Marcus Daly, an emerging Butte mine owner who later developed the smelter in Anaconda. Daly, Paris Gibson (a wealthy Great Falls businessman) and others pointed out the potential of the Great Falls area for power generation and smelting operations. Hill, recognizing the growing importance of Butte's mining industry, wanted a rail connection to that city. He promised Daly "all the transportation you want...."

In order to secure this traffic while the StPM&M's construction trains were still 800 miles away, Hill organized the Montana Central and surveyed a line between Great Falls and Butte via Helena and the Boulder Valley. Colonel Charles Broadwater, a Helena hotel owner and investor, became president of the supposedly independent road. Track laying was completed to Helena on November 16, 1887, and to Butte in 1888.

This 1912 view shows a southbound Great Northern (Montana Central) passenger train at Wickes about a mile north of the Boulder Tunnel. The Northern Pacific obtained trackage rights over GN's line sometime after 1896.

G.N. Ry.
LOOP & CUT AT
WICKES, MONT. 2-25-12.

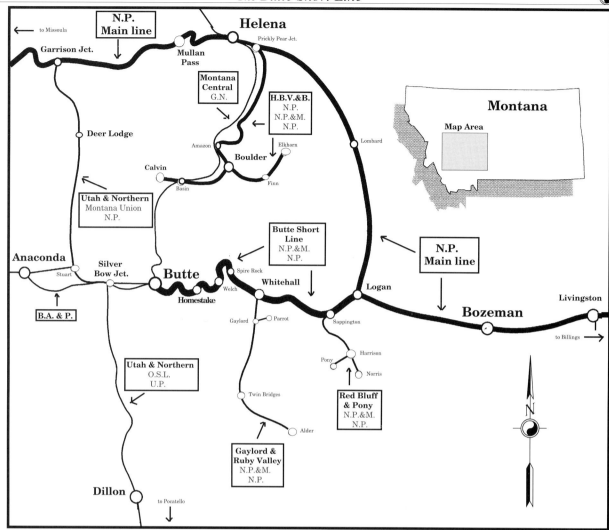

The map above illustrates the railroad lines constructed in southwest Montana between 1880 and 1910. The company constructing the line is shown in black, and subsequent owners or operators are shown in gray.

Simultaneously with Hill's 60th birthday and the statehood of Montana and other northwest territories in 1889, the StPM&M, the MC and other properties were reorganized under the mantle of the Great Northern. They were operated as one railroad. As Hill planned to resume his construction west, he looked at extending the line on from Butte, but he ultimately rejected this and other proposed choices in favor of a route directly west from Havre.

Hill later assisted Marcus Daly in the construction of a railroad to connect the mines in Butte with a new smelter in Anaconda. This railroad would become the

The invitation above was issued to John S. Prince to attend the opening celebration of the MC in Helena on Monday, November 21, 1887.

A 1980 view of the south portal of the Boulder Tunnel at Amazon on the Montana Central. The tunnel's elevation is 6,145' above sea level.

Butte, Anaconda and Pacific. The GN operated the BA&P during 1892, its first year.

There were now two railroads with branch lines into Butte, but the NP had only interchange rights at Garrison and felt it might lose those.

The NP Looks Toward Butte

By 1886 it seemed as though the agreement between the UP and the NP concerning Butte was going to break down. Competitive construction between the two roads was breaking out in Washington. Faced with the possible failure of its agreement with the UP, the new competition presented by Hill's Montana Central surveying south from Great Falls, and the continuing pressure of the Butte businessmen, the NP once again contemplated construction to Butte while remaining firmly committed to its Helena main line. General Adna Anderson, chief engineer, recommended construction toward the mining city on two fronts.

First, a line was planned from Garrison to Butte paralleling the U&N route. Second, a line was surveyed south from Helena to compete with the Montana Central's Boulder Valley route.

While the NP board of directors approved the construction of both lines, they tried negotiations first. In 1886 the NP and UP successfully concluded an agreement concerning the U&N's Garrison-Butte/Anaconda lines. A new UP/NP company, owned jointly, would be formed to operate this trackage. It would be named the Montana Union.

The Montana Union

The 1886 agreement stated the UP would standard gauge its U&N track from Garrison to Butte in lieu of laying a third rail. It would lease the line to the newly formed Montana Union for 999 years. The MU would also handle the business resulting from construction of Daly's new smelter complex in Anaconda. Railroad equipment would be pooled; all revenue and expenses would be shared by both roads.

On a single day--July 24, 1887--the entire northern part of the U&N from Pocatello to Garrison Jct. was converted to standard gauge by prepositioned UP construction crews and equipment.

The NP now had direct albeit shared line into Butte via the Montana Union. Its relationship with the Union Pacific, however, remained fragile.

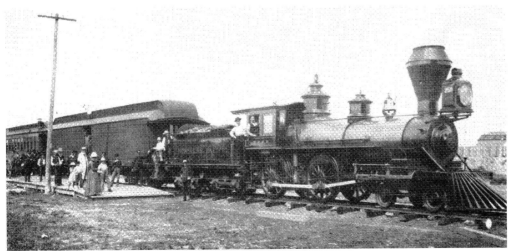

The first NP passenger train over the Montana Union stands at the MU depot in Butte, headed by locomotive #350. On a single day--July 24, 1887--the UP standard gauged the entire U&N north of Pocatello as a result of their agreement with the NP.

PHP

An NP freighthouse and yard facility were built in Butte, and by late 1886 Garrison had become an important interchange point for traffic going to and coming from Butte via the NP mainline.

In 1889, however, the Interstate Commerce Commission ruled that pooled traffic such as that on the Montana Union forestalled competitive trade and was therefore illegal. The UP & NP would need to compete. This ruling resulted in the two parent roads becoming rivals for traffic on the jointly owned MU. Conflict resulted, still the MU continued to exist until 1898.

The UP/NP partnership would end for a number of reasons, but an important one was that Marcus Daly became angry with the MU over poor service and freight rates for shipping Anaconda ore in the 1880's. He moved all Anaconda traffic to the BA&P upon the completion of that road in 1892.

Both the UP and NP went into bankruptcy in 1893. Because the NP completed reorganization in 1896, two years before the UP, it was able to obtain sole possession of the 999 year lease on the Butte to Garrison line.

But until then, the successful formation of the MU meant the NP's attention could now turn to its second attempt to reach Butte on its own rails. The Helena & Jefferson County would extend south from Jefferson City through the Boulder Valley to Butte via Elk Park to compete with the Montana Central. Later a line would be built west up the Jefferson Valley from Three Forks and north along the Boulder River to Boulder. Once built, these new lines would accomplish a number of strategic goals which were to the advantage of the NP.

Northern Pacific & Montana

Under its original charter the NP could not construct branch lines, but it could buy existing roads. Consequently, railroads which would later become NP branches were built during the 1880's, financed by private parties (particularly Samuel T. Hauser, a Helena banker) in association with the NP. Railroad officials themselves often invested.

In 1889 these corporate entities were deeded to the Northern Pacific & Montana, a holding company. As part of the reorganization of 1896 and changes in the law, the NP&M properties were absorbed by the Northern Pacific.

Helena, Boulder Val. & Butte

One of the several lines built this way was the Hauser financed Helena, Boulder Valley & Butte Railroad. This was to be NP's second front in the Butte access struggle. It would give the NP a company owned line into that city, it would block the Montana Central and counter the threat posed by the Hill interests, and it would contribute to Helena remaining as an important economic and railroad center.

Beginning in 1886, the NP began to survey south from Jefferson City and the previously constructed Helena & Jefferson County which served the smelter at Wickes. The new line would go via Boulder Hill, Boulder, Basin, and Calvin.

The Montana Central's survey paralleled the NP's the whole way. The major difference was that the MC planned to build a mile-long tunnel through Boulder Hill while the NP contented itself with a steep, curvy grade over the 6,600+ foot summit called the "Sky Line." Until the Boulder Tunnel was completed in 1888, the MC operated over NP's "Sky Line." In turn the NP used its own mountain grade until after 1896 when it obtained trackage rights over the MC, through their

Both the Montana Central and the HBV&B passed through Basin. The MC depot is at center left in this view taken about 1910. The camera looks west up the Boulder River toward Calvin and Bernice.

Boulder Tunnel. By 1887 both roads had reached Calvin (Bernice on the MC) five miles west of Basin and 17 miles north of Butte.

The Montana Central secured its right-of-way up Bison Creek, across Elk Park on the continental divide and down Woodville Hill into Butte first, however, which made the NP's construction along that same survey very difficult. The NP's grade would need to cross the MC's in Elk Park and descend the steep hill into Butte via a 4% grade with tight corners and a high bridge. Then it would cross the MC 's yard tracks in Butte to get to its terminal.

In addition, before its completion in 1888, the Montana Central was required to enter into last minute litigation against John Legget, operator of the Gambetta Mine, over the ownership of the MC's right-of-way through the property. The settlement of this case required the MC to relocate its line above Meaderville. The implications of this suit on the NP's survey were never tested, but it probably would have led to similar results. All this was to have a direct impact on the HBV&B as it attempted to complete its line from Calvin to Butte--something that was never done.

Politics, Tunnel & Coal

It would require a separate book to explain the nuances of politics that led to the abandonment of the Northern Pacific's Calvin-Butte extension in favor of a different route. Let it suffice to say that Butte was becoming the most influential city in the state, and the growing mine traffic made it an increasingly lucrative market for whatever railroad had access to it. By 1888 three railroads had lines into Butte -- The Utah & Northern, the Montana Union and the recently completed Montana Central. But each was a branch, and what Butte needed was main line service to bring coal in and take mining products out.

Another branch line operation, such as that proposed by the HBV&B was not what the mine owners wanted, even with the proposed Boulder to Jefferson River connection. What they needed was a through route, particularly with connections to the east. They were willing to pull political strings within the NP to build over the Pipestone route surveyed by the Butte Board of Trade rather than to complete the HBV&B. As a "clear headed business man of this city" (maybe Wm. Clark?) stated in a *Butte Semi-Weekly Miner* interview dated January 18, 1888,

The company [NP] wanted a line to Butte, and to one not acquainted with the circumstances, it might seem a very peculiar move on their part to build that line, not by the natural open way up the valleys of the Jefferson and Pipestone, but by a series of ups and downs by steep grades and a tremendous amount of curvature over the bunch of mountains between Helena and Butte.

The Butte Board of Trade would get some help from nature and from a coal discovery south of Billings.

In 1887 one hundred feet of the NP's Mullan Tunnel west of Helena caved in. Mining magnate Marcus Daly himself supervised the repair. In 1888 the tunnel's western snowshed burned. Both events closed the tunnel for several weeks necessitating the relaying of rail on the old switchback line. This virtually eliminated heavy eastern shipments to and from Butte via the Montana Union. Many people questioned

the route's viability, particularly people in Butte. While it could never be abandoned, there was nothing to preclude the NP from building a second main line through Butte. Given recent experiences with the Mullan Tunnel, an alternative main line was, in fact, something desireable. The resistance had always been from General Anderson and the NP leadership, but that leadership was soon to change and with it would change the NP's commitment to Helena and the HBV&B.

Rocky Fork & Cooke City

Marcus Daly's new Washoe smelter in Anaconda and other smelter operations in Butte required huge amounts of clean burning coal. This coal had always been brought in on the UP from the Wyoming coal fields. In fact, the 1886 Montana Union agreement gave the UP exclusive rights to supply coal to the area served by the MU, and it prohibited the NP from entering that market. Wyoming coal, however, was of inferior quality. Daly began to look around for another source of supply and the means to provide it.

The MU had never really been able to keep up with the tonnage requirements of the Anaconda smelter because of its shoddy track, dilapidated equipment, and the steep grade from Stuart to Anaconda. Daly complained, and the UP began to pressure the NP to contribute more in order to up-

No. _____ May 20 1889
RECEIVED OF Rocky Fork & Cooke City Railway Co.,
Per A J Me____
Six and _____ 20/100 DOLLARS,
For Services May 1889
DUPLICATE
$6.20
Witness O H Knatt
his
Jno + Byrne
mark

grade the system. The UP even began to survey a new line to Anaconda from Durant via Gregson that would later become the route of the BA&P.

In 1888 a consortium of Montana investors, including ex-governor Samuel T. Hauser, bought a new coal field south of Billings near Red Lodge. They also bought and completed the Rocky Fork and Cooke City which connected Red Lodge with the NP at Laurel. This could deliver superior coal to the Butte and Anaconda markets.

To what degree Daly was a factor in this development is unclear, but Hauser and Daly had cooperated on several other business deals during the period. The charter which lists the investors in the RF&CC and the company which developed the coal fields, however, includes several interesting Northern Pacific names such as vice-president Thomas Oakes, ex-president Henry Villard and lawyer Samuel Word.

In 1888 Kendrick replaced General Anderson as NP's chief engineer for the Rocky Mountain Region, and Oakes became president at a time of prosperity for the NP. New routes were being proposed, and Kendrick was given control over NP construction in Montana. He was known to favor "short lines."

It was obvious to Kendrick (who also was in private negotiations with Daly for a Northern Pacific line to Anaconda from

---

The principal object of the road, Mr. Kendrick admitted, was to get the coal of the Rocky Fork company into this market. It has already been announced in the THE MINER that a syndicate composed of Villard, Haggin, Oakes, Hauser and others has bought the Rocky Fork Company out and propose to enter the markets of the Northwest with a first-class article of fuel at a price that will make it impractible for other coal companies to compete with it.

Butte Semi-Weekly Miner   **February 2, 1889**

THE DAILY INDEPENDENT: HELENA   FEBRUARY 23, 1889

The Boulder Canyon Route

Sentinel: The party under Messrs. Forshay and McHenry, division engineers of the Northern Pacific railroad, which left here last November, are now on their return to this place on a survey via the Jefferson canyon.... The Northern Pacific engineers will be here in a few weeks if everything works in a smooth manner. From a reliable source it was stated yesterday that in the construction department of the Northern Pacific the advisability of adopting the Pipestone pass for the new branch into Butte is under discussion, with fair prospects of this line route being decided upon. In this event the Boulder and Gallatin recently staked out will probably be abandoned. Some immediate action will be taken, however, as a short line to Butte for the transportation of Rocky Fork coal will soon have to be constructed.

Butte that never panned out), that the Calvin route with its grades, curves and longer distances was inadequate, even if the Boulder River line was added to the HBV&B. Kendrick authorized new surveys, although the NP remained publically committed to the Calvin extension.

In November, 1888, division engineers E.H. McHenry and Forshay were directed to find a new, more direct route into Butte. McHenry re-surveyed the Butte Board of Trade's route over Pipestone Pass, but concluded Homestake Pass four miles to the north was 80 feet lower and five

---

THE DAILY INDEPENDENT: HELENA   April 12, 1889

THE BUTTE LINE

Engineer Kendrick Says the Northern Pacific Has Selected the Homestake Pass

It Will Cost Much Less Than the Pipestone, and Will Be Completed by November 20

BUTTE, April 11. -- [Special to the Independent.] -- A meeting of the board of trade committee and the Northern Pacific engineers in regard to the Pipestone Pass survey was held this afternoon in the office of N.C. Ray. Northern Pacific representatives were J.W. Kendrick, chief engineer of the Northern Pacific, Engineers McHenry and Haven and Agent McCaig. Mr. Kendrick said that after careful examination of all the routes and a consideration of Ray's report on the Pipestone, he had definitely determined to locate the Northern Pacific line to Butte over the Homestake pass. This pass is a few miles north of the Pipestone, and Mr. Kendrick stated that it is eighty feet lower at the summit. He also made the statement that it offers a route between Butte and Three Forks six miles shorter than the Pipestone Pass, and can be built at a saving of $142,000 over the Pipestone route. The result is entirely acceptable to the business men of Butte, as the Homestake and Pipestone passes are only four miles apart, and a line over either of them will make the Jefferson and Ruby valleys tributary to Butte, and open up a hitherto undeveloped mining district.

Mr. Kendrick left at 2 o'clock, intending to go straight through to St. Paul. He informed your correspondent that he had ordered the rails for the line by telegraph, and intended to have the road from Three Forks to Butte in operation Nov. 20. He said he chose the Homestake route because it was the best and cheapest, and denied with great emphasis that any improper means were used to locate the main line of the Northern Pacific by way of Mullan Pass.

miles shorter than Pipestone. It was the most direct route for Rocky Fork coal into Butte. By February two hundred NP surveyors were staking out the new line which would leave the main line at Canyon House (Logan), follow the Jefferson River to its junction with Big Pipestone Creek, up that stream west for seven miles, climb Homestake Creek to the summit at Homestake Pass and descend into Butte.

The formal announcement of the route was made to the press April 11, 1889. Keefe and Greene, the same contractors who built the RF&CC would be the general contractors for what would become known as the Butte Short Line. Keefe would supervise construction on the west side and Green would supervise on the east side. Before construction could begin, however, complications with the Union Pacific needed to be resolved. The UP, through its U&N subsidiary, had surveyed a line from Dillon to Helena through the Jefferson Canyon in 1881. Some grading had taken place and the route had been filed in Washington DC. The UP became suspicious of the NP's intentions regarding this route and sent crews to occupy the grade. Before this could be resolved, violence would break out.

The NP planned to complete the HBV&B as far as public statements were concerned, but it would never be finished. Neither the Calvin extension nor the Boulder River line was ever built. Interest in them soon faded away. The NP tracks over Boulder Hill were abandoned in favor of trackage rights over the Montana Central.

In 1889 the mines at Elkhorn looked promising and the NP extended a branch from Boulder to Elkhorn that was completed in 1890. It was also built by Keefe & Green. It was done just in time to see the mines shut down. They re-opened in 1891, but service remained intermittent.

By 1907 the Calvin branch was abandoned back to Boulder. In 1931 the Elkhorn line was scrapped, and the Northern Pacific retired from the Boulder Valley altogether. The HBV&B which began with such great promise was no more.

A Helena, Boulder Valley & Butte mixed train with Haynes' photo car makes its way downgrade around the loop near Queen Siding on its way from Elkhorn to Boulder in 1895. This line was completed in 1889 after efforts to reach Butte via the Boulder Valley were abandoned. Mine closures saw service on this line discontinued almost immediately, but service was reinstituted in 1891 when the mines reopened. The branch would linger until 1931.

MHS

2. Building the Short Line

The Union Pacific's Response

Union Pacific officials watched the Northern Pacific's maneuvering to build directly into Butte with interest. As long as the NP was just contemplating another branch line over difficult terrain the UP remained quiet, but in 1888 the UP's perception of the Butte railroad scene changed.

First, Marcus Daly announced in 1888 he was going to build his own railroad between Butte and Anaconda, and there were rumors he was negotiating with both Hill and Kendrick. Since a great deal of the traffic on the Montana Union was Daly's, the UP would suffer accordingly.

Second, the development of the Rocky Fork coal fields near Red Lodge and the building of the RF&CC by NP interests threatened the coal monopoly the UP enjoyed with the Butte mines and the Anaconda smelter. If a shorter line could be built from the east by which Rocky Fork's superior coal could be hauled into Butte more cheaply, the UP would be the loser.

Third, the successful construction of a short line by the NP between Three Forks and Butte as announced by Kendrick would give the NP a virtual main line through Butte because of its sharing of the MU to Garrison. This would place the UP at a disadvantage since the UP entered the city over a 150 mile branch line which crossed the continental divide twice.

These three developments jarred the UP out of its complacency. It began almost immediately to survey a new line to Anaconda via Gregson Springs and to pressure the NP to increase its contribution toward upgrading the Montana Union to pacify Daly. It then looked east to the Jefferson River Valley.

In 1881 the Utah & Northern had surveyed a route from Dillon to Helena when its plans had still included building to that city. The survey followed a water level route through Twin Bridges, Jefferson Canyon, Three Forks and along the Missouri River. Fifteen miles of grading had been completed and the survey filed in Washington when the 1882 agreement between the U&N and the NP led to a junction between them at Garrison instead.

The route had seen no action since, but in the spring of 1889, the UP put out surveyors once again expressing "as much interest to reach Helena as the Northern Pacific has to reach Butte." They indicated this might be part of a broader scheme to link the U&N with the OR&N west of Missoula. When asked if this might not break the Montana Union agreement with the NP, UP attorney Sam Word said,

> I think it will. The Union Pacific does not care for that agreement because the Northern Pacific has never lived up to it. The Northern Pacific has never put up the money for the improvements required by that agreement and I think it will fall to the ground at once.

War on the Jefferson

On February 1, 1889, the Union Pacific started work on the middle section of the Helena line through the strategic Jefferson Canyon by repairing the old grade. While there was room for two roads through the canyon (20 years later the Milwaukee would build through here on the other side of the river), there was no doubt it would make the NP's surveying of a line through this narrow defile more difficult.

The Northern Pacific's response was swift. While President Oakes urged caution and renewed negotiations with the UP to up-grade the Montana Union, J.W. Kendrick put men in the field. On March 2, 1889, NP surveyors under E.H. McHenry physically removed UP graders from their line in the Jefferson Canyon and occupied the property. Reports differ as to the extent of the violence used by the "surveyors" to accomplish this task, but no one appears to have been injured.

On March 5th, 210 Union Pacific "graders" with a supply of "150 pick handles" under chief engineer Bogue arrived in Boulder on the Montana Central and set off for the Jefferson Canyon. Along with them was a deputy sheriff to give the operation some semblance of legality. Helena's *Daily Independent* said, "A conflict is inevitable, and sensational, if not alarming reports, are looked for from the Jefferson canyon." The UP force evicted the NP group and reoccupied the line. Again, there were no apparent injuries. Before the level of violence could escalate again, however, calmer heads prevailed, and a negotiated settlement was reached between the two companies.

The *Daily Independent* outlined the plan on March 16th. The Northern Pacific would immediately take possession of the canyon and complete the grade already started by the UP. The NP agreed to pay the UP $28,596.00 for the work they had completed. Furthermore, it was agreed that if the UP built its Helena line within five years, the NP would give it trackage rights through the canyon. If not, the NP would get the line forever. The agreement held, and the Union Pacific withdrew from the Jefferson Valley. Its line to Helena was never built. By April 11, 1889, the survey was completed, and the Northern Pacific was ready to award contracts.

JEFFERSON CANYON

THE ABSURD CANARDS OF A WAR THERE DISSIPATED

The Facts as Regards the Union Pacific's Possession Since 1881 - Steps Taken by the Road to Retain Its Rights in Jefferson Canyon

E.C. Kinney, the resident engineer of the Union Pacific road, returned Friday afternoon from the Jefferson Canyon, where the supposed war between the Union and Northern Pacific roads has been in progress. When asked as to the status of the "combatants," he laughed out and said he had been amused by the fuss raised by the press over nothing. It is bosh about the Union Pacific having sent an armed body of men to retake possession of their work in the canyon. The facts are these:

The line of the Union Pacific from Dillon to Helena was surveyed and a charter granted for it in 1881. This was before the Northern Pacific reached the Territory. The papers claiming the right of way were filed in Washington and Helena in compliance with statutory requirements. About $125,000 was expended upon the work of grading the line of which about $50,000 was laid out in the Jefferson Canyon . Altogether there were about fifteen miles graded. But the Northern Pacific was heading direct for Butte, and both roads came to a mutual understanding on the subject. The Union Pacific agreed to complete its line of the Utah & Northern to Garrison while the Northern Pacific agreed to abstain from coming directly into Butte but went by Helena instead. Each road thus had indirect access to the points in the Territory it aimed at to enter directly. The Union Pacific allowed the work on its intended line to Helena to remain in status quo, but the rights it possessed remained intact because the proper legal officer had never taken steps to have them declared lapsed. But with the entrance of the Montana Central into Butte a new factor presented itself which proposed to take away the Butte field entirely from the Northern Pacific. It became necessary for the preservation of the existence of that road, as far as regards Butte business, that it should have direct entrance to Butte. When this intention was made public, the Union Pacific concluded to complete the line to Helena from Glen, properly speaking, on the U&N. In order to lose no time, Resident engineer Kinney was directed to go ahead with the rock work in Jefferson Canyon and restore the work already done there which had become out of repair through its remaining untouched for several years. Accordingly, about thirty days ago Mr. Kinney put a party of thirty or forty men on this work. They were strung over the six miles of the canyon in parties of three or four men each, when the Northern Pacific decided to endeavor to get possession of the work done by the Union Pacific.

The Northern Pacific had surveyed a line through the canyon but had filed no papers at Washington claiming a right of way. There is plenty of room in the canyon for it to parallel the Union Pacific line on the same side of the river, and just as much room on the other side to run a similar line to that held by the Union Pacific. But here was a chance to save fifty thousand dollars worth of work. So a party of fifty men or so was sent in before whom the small parties of the Union Pacific had to retire one after another. When this became known to Engineer Kinney, he collected about 150 men here and in Helena, and before such a force as this, the Northern Pacific party had no alternative but to retreat.

"We didn't want any fighting." said Mr. Kinney. "It is all bosh about our sending bands of armed men there to retake our ground. I would not put guns into the hands of such men as I sent in there under any circumstances. We had a few guns, probably half a dozen shotguns, in the hands of the men in charge of the gang. We proceeded perfectly legally. We had a Deputy Sheriff of Jefferson county in charge to enforce our lawful rights and maintain the preservation of peace. I told him we did not want any fighting. We said to the Northern Pacific men, 'This is our ground. We want it and have the force to get it if necessary to exert it.' They saw the force of the argument and moved away."

"And have you now possession of all the Union Pacific right of way in the canyon?"

"All but a mile or so. We think we will take it when we want though, of course. I don't want to be understood as making any blow about it. It's just the same as in the case of a private individual whose title to a piece of ground is clear. He has a right to use force, if necessary, to maintain his possession. The Northern Pacific has not right as yet in the canyon, having filed no papers in Washington setting forth the ground it claims, while the Union Pacific has. Therefore, the latter has got rights to enforce - peaceably if we can; forcibly if we must. The few guns in our party are more for effect than for use. I sent over 150 pick handles for the boys, and told them to pound the other fellows with them if they didn't give way peaceably, but they were not required."

The construction of this line from Dillon may alter the line of the Utah & Northern from Melrose. From Dillon its course is down the Jefferson river to the Missouri river. The Big Hole joins the Jefferson at Twin Bridges, and by building a link from Twin Bridges to Glen the Utah & Northern may be rerouted.....

Butte Semi-Weekly Miner   **March 13, 1889**

The NP Awards the Contract

In April of 1889 the NP called for bids on the proposed line. The bid sheet listed the project as just over 69 miles in length, a summit tunnel of just under 1,000 feet, and at least three major bridges including crossings of both the Madison and Jefferson Rivers. Projected cost would be around $2,000,000.

For three or four weeks major contractors and their representatives toured the route. They all admitted it would be a difficult and expensive line to build. It would be especially difficult on the east side where the terrain was so rough.

Bids were submitted, and on May 18, 1889, the contract was awarded to Green, Barbour & Co. aka Keefe & Green, the same firm which was finishing the RF&CC. Coincidentally with building the new short line to Butte the firm would also build a new branch from Boulder to Elkhorn on the HBV&B and a branch to Norris and Pony -- to be known as the Red Bluff and Pony Railroad. The latter would leave the Butte line at Sappington.

Mr. Keefe had been so confident his firm would get the bid that he bet another contractor $5,000 on the outcome. In addition, his crews had already graded two miles of right-of-way before the award was announced.

Part of Mr. Keefe's confidence might have come from the fact that Keefe, Green and Barbour were associates of S.T. Hauser of Helena. Hauser was in business with A.B. Hammond and E.L. Bonner. All were partners in

THE CONTRACT AWARDED

HELENA PARTIES TO BUILD THE HOMESTAKE BRANCH

Northern Pacific Directors Meet and Give the Work to Greene, Barbour & Co. The figures at Which the Award was Made Said to be the Lowest Ever Submitted for Similar Work in the West.

Private dispatches were received from New York yesterday afternoon which stated that the directors of the Northern Pacific had met in regular monthly session and had awarded the contract for the construction of the Homestake pass branch to Butte, to Greene, Barbour & Co. of Helena.

It cannot be said that the other bidders were surprised at the result, as Mr. Keefe has made a boast during the last six weeks that he would show the Minnesota contractors some figures on construction work that would "paralyze 'em," and he evidently has been as good as his word. It is understood that the figures at which the award has been made are very low, in fact the lowest that have ever been submitted for railroad work in the west. The different classifications of work, it is said, will show a reduction of 20 per cent, when compared with those paid by the Montana Central.

Work will begin immediately at both ends of the line -- Butte and Canon House Junction, near Gallatin. It is the intention of the chief engineer to build about fifteen miles from this end, which comprises all of the heavy work.

The time set for the completion of the branch is January 1, 1890.

Butte Semi-Weekly Miner   May 18, 1889

the Montana Improvement Company, as was Marcus Daly. The trio had financed several Montana railroad projects for the NP including the Missoula and Bitter Root Valley and the Drummond and Philipsburg. Hauser was a partner in the RF&CC. In fact, Hauser had been the agent for NP construction in Montana since 1882. Bonner was in St. Paul when the NP board of directors awarded the contract for the Butte Short Line. It is little wonder that Keefe felt so confident.

The Butte Short Line was to be a project of the new Northern Pacific & Montana. Hammond and Bonner provided the bonds for the project. Marcus Daly initially invested $10,000, but he sold out when he and Hammond got into a wide-ranging feud over Hammond's politics during the 1889 Montana statehood election.

Construction workers carve out the right-of-way on the west side of Homestake Pass in 1889 near what would later become Skones. During this era the place was known as Dead Woman's Cabin. Mr. Keefe of Keefe and Green supervised this section. Subcontractors were Drum and Breckenridge who had some labor troubles on this part of the line which resulted in the burning of an Italian workers' camp.   JVM

Last Minute Maneuvering

Construction began in June, 1889, and the contracted completion date was January 1, 1890. Keefe & Green were the general contractors, but they subcontracted much of the work.

Keefe supervised the crews working on the west side and Green did the same for the east side. Matthews & Co. had the bridge contract. The bridge building was an awesome task involving the construction of over 70 structures containing millions of board feet of lumber.

Some litigation was necessary first, however. The Montana Central and the NP clashed over a site for terminal tracks in Butte. The two roads occupied adjacent yard facilities on Nevada Street, but the MC owned much of the land between them. The NP needed this land including the ground designated for the Montana Central depot.

The NP brought suit against the MC saying it should be sold some of the MC land to expand its terminal, given the proposed increase in traffic over the new Gallatin line. In May, 1889, the court ruled in favor of the NP saying "the Northern Pacific gets the land as it has the greater public necessity." The MC took the case to the Supreme Court.

When people in Butte learned the NP was changing their survey to enter Butte from the east, many rushed out to file mining claims along the Pipestone route figuring the NP would utilize the Ray survey over that pass. They hoped the NP would have to pay them large sums for title to these claims. McHenry was credited by the Butte press with being particularly wily in keeping the actual route over Homestake a secret for so long thus avoiding the expensive land acquisition costs involved in dispensing with these frivolous claims.

In town this was not so easy. In one case the NP lawyer advised Agent McCaig to have a fence erected around a piece of disputed land near the proposed yard and patrol it with operating personnel. He believed possession would dictate ownership in this case.

The scope of the "Gallatin" project was huge. Construction was slated to be completed within a single building season, and the appropriate logistical support was essential. Enoch Hodson Sawmill in Boulder was awarded a contract for 30,000 ties for example. Another contract was awarded for 60,000 ties for the grade between Canyon House and Jefferson Bar. Ties were cut on the NP right-of-way near Spire Rock, and 8,000,000 feet of lumber was purchased in Missoula County (presumably from the Hammond mill). Quaintance and Leighton of Boulder were given a contract to furnish all the meat used by the Keefe & Green crews (about 4,000 men) at 5.5 cents per pound dressed and delivered.

Labor was in short supply, so labor contractors were contacted and foreign laborers including several hundred Italians worked on the project.

Officially constructed by the NP&M, the road would be given the name the Butte Short Line. The newspapers of the day referred to it as the "Gallatin Branch." It would be operated as a branch of the Northern Pacific Railroad.

Construction Begins

Construction proceeded rapidly from both ends of the new line simultaneously. Green was able to utilize the former UP grade through Jefferson Canyon, so primary attention was paid to the part from Butte to the summit (about ten miles) because of its difficulty of construction. It was estimated by Keefe that they could have the line from Butte to the summit done in 60 days utilizing 1,000 Italian workers employed by sub-contractors Drum & Breckenridge.

Both approaches to the summit tunnel were completed by July 13, 1889, and the *Butte Miner* for that date reported good progress to the foot of the hill on the east side.

Construction was not without mishap. On July 14th two Italian workers were killed when some black powder exploded on the west side above "Dead Woman's Cabin" near what would later be known as Skones siding.

The *Butte Miner* reported on July 27th the "second fatal accident in two days" when ten miles east of Homestake summit foreman Rasmussen of Touhy Brothers (subcontractors on the east side) was killed. He had gone to examine a charge that misfired, and it exploded in his face. There are several accounts in the local press of this type of accident happening.

In November Touhys' would suffer another loss while blasting near Spire Rock. One shot went off. The men returned to set a second charge when a violent explosion killed John Dell, A.W. Larson, Tom O'Cleary and Horn Ross. Con

Sullivan was thrown 200 feet through the air and subsequently died. Another worker was blinded.

In April, 1890, Francis Ratelle brought suit against Keefe & Green for $25,000 and costs for injuries suffered the previous year as a worker.

In August falling rock in the summit tunnel severed the leg of one Italian worker and injured another. The first man was brought to Butte but died from loss of blood. As a result of this and other accidents on the west side, some labor difficulty broke out with the Italians working for Drum & Breckenridge. Despite these difficulties the *Butte Miner* speculated, "New Year's Day would hear locomotive whistles blow in Butte."

By September 14, 1889, 27 miles were completed from the east end and five miles were completed from the Butte end. This left 39 miles to do, but the contractors promised 22 would be completed by the 22nd.

By October 5th trains were running on both ends of the line delivering nearly all of the supplies and materials.

36 miles of track have been ironed on the east end from Canyon House [Logan] where the road leaves the mainline toward Jefferson.

reported the *Miner*. Four miles had been reportedly "ironed" on the west end. The tunnel construction was expected to be done in four weeks. The railroad hoped to turn the line over to the operating department by December 15th.

In October the first passengers traveled over the line when picnickers from Three Forks and Willow Creek arranged a trip to Pipestone Springs, a developing recreation site on the east side of the continental divide. Livestock was shipped east as soon as the line was finished to Whitehall.

Construction of terminal facilities in Butte, however, lagged behind as did the bridge build-

---

The Butte Miner   July 12, 1889

Into Death's Mouth

A GALLANT BAND WHICH PERFORMED MOST NOBLE AND VALOUROUS SERVICE

Graphic and Thrilling Account by the Miner's War Correspondent of a Fierce and Terrific Battle Fought Near the City Yesterday - The Miner, the Only Paper to Have a Representative on the Field.

There is at least one contracting firm in Montana to-day which has had more than its fill of cheap foreign labor. That firm is Drum & Breckinridge on the line of the Butte Short Line, or the Northern Pacific & Montana railroad, as it is officially known.

When Keefe, Green took the contract of building the line, they feared a scarcity of labor in the territory and went to an employment agency at St. Paul for a gang of Italians. They arrived and were assigned to Drum & Breckinridge sub-contractors, who are building a portion of the grade about six miles from town. For a while all went well until the man Tarcinali was killed by a sliding rock, last Sunday. This put the gang in a bad humor as they blamed, although unjustly, the foreman for the accident. Since then they have been surly and ill humored. The discharge of four or five of their compatriots during the past two or three days, for general incompeting and laziness has not tended to mollify their haughty Roman spirits, and, if anything, they became worse. Yesterday morning another one was discharged, whereupon a portion of the remaining ones quit work and compelled a number of others who refused to join them to quit also. They next waited upon the contractors and told them that unless the discharged man was reinstated all would strike. Their request was not complied with, and the mob, about 100 of them, became exceedingly boisterous and threatening, and all were discharged. Mr. Drum informed Mr. Keefe of what had transpired, and upon his advice came to town and notified the authorities. In the absence of Mr. De Witt, Acting Prosecuting Attorney Corbett instructed Sheriff Lloyd to visit the scene of the disturbance with a posse and see that no violations of the law were committed.

The Sheriff at once organized a posse of five men...started out in Lavelle's band wagon drawn by four horses. All were armed with Winchesters and a look of determination.... When within a few hundred yards of the camp General Lloyd went ahead to reconnoiter.... The camp, composed of tents and wickiups...at once began to swarm with ... Italians and all crowded around the valorous [group]. General Lloyd acted as spokesman and ... stated that complaint had been made to him that the men whom he was addressing had behaved in a rude and boisterous manner calculated to incite riot, war, bloodshed, agony and death, and then told them that his orders were from the contractors to clean out the camp and cause every last man from Italy to vamoose the ranch. Their ambassador bluntly said, "No cleana the campa outa 'till we get our mon. 'Merican bossa he go to towna, he discharga Italiana mana and we wanta oura mon." They were then informed by the sheriff that if they would leave peaceably and go to town he would see that they would receive their "mon,"....

Mr Breckinridge now appeared and introducing himself to General Lloyd stated that his partner, Mr. Drum, was still in town and that if the men would also go to town they would receive their time checks.

All this time the remainder of the ... posse were in the wagon, and seeing their comrades surrounded...caused the driver to take them into the camp, and as soon as they arrived they jumped out with a gun in each hand. Hurriedly handing one to General Lloyd, Captain Kessler...and others formed themselves into open columns, threw out skirmish lines and waited for the signal which was to announce that the battle should begin. The sight of so large an army, equipped and armed for a protracted campaign, caused the vassals to weaken and they became less defiant, and some made a pretense of packing up and preparing to leave the camp.

Seeing they were no longer inclined to make trouble, Mr. Breckinridge requested the General to leave a part of his posse as guard, and he would allow the mob to remain on the ground until this morning, when he would send them to town to get their pay. The General consented.... The trio had gone a mile or two when they met Mr. Drum going toward the camp.... He informed the commanding officer that he was ready to settle with the men, and that as soon as he got back to the seat of war he would give every last one of them their time checks and "fire them."

Upon receipt ... General Lloyd ... countermarched and in a short time ...was once more collected together in the presence of the demoralized enemy. The General ordered the camp cleared....

In an instant the enemy began to pack.... While this was going on the General issued an order to take down all the tents which belonged to the contractor, and load them into a convenient wagon.... When the last wickiup was also emptied, the match was applied and in a moment they were blazing as only the pitchy mountain pine can burn.... Mr. Drum, who was in a cabin, about a quarter of a mile away, ordered a squad of [workers] to advance to the same place and receive their time checks....

In a little while every one of the strikers was paid off and a couple of the firm's teamsters loaded all the baggage onto wagons and brought it to South Butte....

Thus ended probably one of the fiercest and most notable battles between civilized and uncivilized men ever fought in the territory; not even excepting Camas Creek or the Battle of the Big Hole.

MHS

F.J. Haynes took a hand car ride over the Butte Short Line soon after its completion in 1890. This photo is captioned "BSL, trestle no. 74, Montana." It is a photo of the bridge just west of Homestake Tunnel and is an example of the estimated three and one half miles of wooden bridge work done over Homestake Pass by Matthews & Co. of St. Paul. Their delay held up the final completion date. This and about 40 other bridges were filled in as part of a Northern Pacific line improvement program from 1900 to 1902.

ing above Pipestone on the east side. By October 19th the foundation for the roundhouse in Butte was finished, but the engine pits had to be rebuilt when they caved in. The structure would be built from local brick out of Anaconda, reported to be of "high quality." Butte's terminal construction was reported to cost $150,000 alone. But the optimistic statements to the press concerning completion dates for the BSL failed to come true as was often the case in railroad construction.

Bridges Hold Up the Line

Bridges delayed the construction of the line because of their number and inaccessibility. Matthews & Co. had to build over 70 wooden structures which were required to cross the many water courses and valleys found in the rough country along the east side

of the divide. Only primitive wagon roads permitted access to several of the bridge construction sites.

By the end of October rails had been laid on 50 miles of the line, and the east end was beginning to carry some commercial traffic. The summit tunnel was yet to be finished "as well as several million feet of bridge building."

On November 15th, Keefe and Green recognized they were not going to be able to complete the road by January 1st. They moved 1,000 laborers to the Elkhorn branch of the HBV&B in a futile attempt to complete that line by the scheduled date while the bridges were being finished on the BSL. The construction of the Elkhorn branch was going on simultaneously with that of the BSL. This lead to widespread speculation in the press that the

Boulder-Jefferson line was finally going to be built with a connection at Finn siding on the Elkhorn branch, but this was not to be true.

Bridge building continued at a furious pace through December,

The Butte Branch

M.H. Keefe, of the firm of Green, Keefe & Co., who have the contract for building the branch of the Northern Pacific from Three Forks to Butte, was in the city last evening, and gave some particulars of the work now going on. The completion of the road has been delayed by the bridge work in the mountainous part of the line. This, however, is now well under way, and the last rail will be laid on March 25. There will then be 26 miles of surfacing to do, which can be finished at the rate of about a mile a day. During this interval, says the *Anaconda Review*, there will be nothing to interfere with the running of freight trains. It is not likely, however, that the road will be turned over to the operating department before April 15. The contract calls for the completion of every detail of the work, including depots and terminal buildings, by May 1, and the road may not be operated before that date. Trains can be run, however, if necessary, by April 1.

Daily Independent   **Feb 2, 1890**

but the projected completion date was no longer possible. A new finishing date of March 15, 1890, was announced to the press.

The Keefe & Green crews returned from the Elkhorn branch in January. Rails were laid through the tunnel and to the bridges on the east side which were still not finished.

The Line Completed

On March 29, 1890, the rail laying crews from east and west met on bridge 54 five miles east of Homestake. Butte residents were so anxious for the line's completion that, according to the *Daily Independent* of Helena (which was probably a bit prejudiced), "A celebration was held [in Butte] two days before the last spike was driven."

On April 21, 1890, Superintendent G.W. Dickinson's special made the trip over the entire line from Logan to Butte even though 12 miles of it still needed to be ballasted. On board were the project engineers from the Northern Pacific & Montana.

The planned delivery of the road to the operating department was delayed until June 1st, however, despite the joining of the line ceremonies that took place in March. Unfinished work plagued Keefe & Green, and acrimony broke out between them and the NP's engineering department as projected completion dates came and went.

J.C. Patterson, whose camp was at Homestake, in his every-other-day update to E.H. McHenry, said on May 21, 1890,

Bridge 54 over Beef Straight Creek in an 1890 Haynes photo. No map lists a "North Fork of Beef Straight Creek," the description given by C.L. Haig in the article at right. The authors believe the last spike ceremony was conducted on this bridge March 29, 1890. By 1901 this bridge was filled in. Pipestone Rock is in the background. Welch Quarry is a mile up the creek.

MHS

The Butte Daily Miner: Butte, Sunday Morning March 30, 1890

THE LAST SPIKE DRIVEN

The Butte & Gallatin Connection Brought to a Successful Finish

The Great Work Completed Amid the Usual Attendant Ceremonials.

Through the kindness of J.C. Patterson, assistant engineer in charge of the construction of the Butte & Gallatin branch of the Northern Pacific railroad from Logan Junction to Butte, an invitation was extended to a few citizens of this city yesterday to witness the driving of the last spike in the branch, one of the most important yet constructed to Butte since it places it 120 miles nearer to St. Paul than by the Garrison connection with the Northern Pacific and affords it the third direct outlet to the East.

At the construction headquarters of the road an engine with a caboose car attached stood ready for the trip. Some time was consumed waiting for all the guests to arrive, and when they had, the following comprised the party: J.C. Patterson, General Agent McCaig, U.S. Marshal Irvine, Auditor Calderhead of the Montana Union, E.M. Trask, Capt. Lyons, Superintendent O'Brien of the Montana Union, Abe Heyman, Col. Jullien of the Mining Journal, Jean Decker of the Anaconda Standard and a representative of THE MINER. The names of the crew in whose charge this precious human freight was placed are Conductor A.W. Waite, Engineer Walter Towne at the throttle of engine No. 83, Fireman Aleck Martin, Brakemen George Walker and Joseph Robert.

The start was made at 3:05 in a driving storm of fine snow, which served to cast a general mist over the landscape. The day was not the best that could have been selected as far as externals go, and the resultant obscuration of the landscape through which the trip was made was generally regretted.

Shortly after passing the trestle over Silver Bow creek the brakeman called out "East Butte," and to the right lay the as yet unpopulated site of the Northern Pacific addition, northeast of the race track, which in a few months will be a thickly settled suburb.

Then the climb began up the sides of the Rocky mountains to where the summit is reached at the top of Homestake pass. From this city, the line appears like a white chalk mark against the mountain side. A trip over the road reveals something entirely unexpected. The road is a series of deep rock cuts, fills and trestles all the way, testifying to the splendid engineering abilities of E.H. McHenry, the chief engineer of the division, and speaking in tones of deepest

meaning of what the Northern Pacific has done for Butte.

The scenery over the route is grand and picturesque. It presents splendid views of mountain ranges, bottomless gorges, rolling hills, nestling valleys all in successive panorama, ever changing, constantly varying, but generally preserving above and over it all a general air of savage grandeur. It passes over a trackless wilderness in places where even the foot of wild beast never made a trail. In short it is as fine a piece of railroading as is to be found in this country of magnificent railroading feats.

After passing over some hair-raising trestles, the highest of them 116 feet high and 600 long, nearest Homestake tunnel, Precinct 34 is reached, and a dreary, woebegone looking place the scene of this celebrated factor in the politics of last fall presented [*it was an election scandal*]. The celebrated house "with paper pasted over the windows" is gone having been torn down last week. Two other shacks near still remain.

The train then entered the Homestake tunnel, which is 700 feet long, timbered all the way through. This was the summit, and a short distance beyond it is the station, just ten miles from the city. The run there was made in half an hour. Historic scenes were passed in the shape of "Dead Woman's ranch" and Alderman Lewis' wood piles. Beef Straight creek comes into view here, and along its courses is said to be still virgin placer diggings of untold richness. The descent to where the last rail was to be laid is not quite so steep as the ascent on the north side of the tunnel, but the run was made slowly, owing to the unballasted condition of the track. The rails are 67 pound steel and when the road is ballasted, properly for fast travel, it will be one of the best in the country to ride over. Yesterday, even with the rails laid on the ties over the unballasted track, there was no jolting or so little as to be almost unnoticeable.

At last the engine came to a stop, and the occupants of the caboose who had been listening to George Irvine and E.M. Trask swap lies about their early adventures with the Indians about Bannack, while Cap. Lyons varied the monotony with telling how he had jumped Brother Shippen's ranch, got out and stamped about in the chilly atmosphere, watching the laborers surfacing the track. They proceeded on foot to where the last rails were being laid on the trestle over the north fork of Beef

Straight. Frank Sullivan, who was in charge of the gang constructing this part of the line for Matthews Bros. & Carrick, with Chauncey Wordward as boss of the tracklayers, hurried the work forward and at last everything was in readiness.

In the presence of a large crowd, composed of laborers and visitors, General Manager McCaig stepped forward in the center of the trestle and in a few well chosen words sketched the progress of the work to its completion and the benefits that it was to be expected would accrue to Butte. His remarks were loudly cheered when, taking a hammer in both hands he brought it down with all his might and the best intentions in the neighborhood of the iron spike that was to clinch the work. The powerful blow left a deep impression on the stringer while the spike proudly reared its head over the rail. United States Marshal Irvine was standing near him and to him Mr. McCaig handed the hammer with the remark:

"You try it next, George. Let's see how well you can miss it."

And Mr. Irvine hauled off and made a dent on the stringer right alongside of Mr. McCaig's. Mr. Calderhead essayed to hit the spike, but it laughed him to scorn and still surveyed with calm indifference. The situation was now growing serious. Mr. Calderhead nervously handed the hammer to Col. Nick O'Brien, who spat on his hands, and casting a wary look round out the northeast corner of his weather eye, remarked:

"Stand clear boys. She's going in this time if the trestle doesn't come down."

With a practiced hand the young Titan raised the hammer aloft and brought it down with a loud twang that lowered the arrogance of that spike three inches, while the next blow sent it with a clang home to its last resting place against the rail.

Abe Heyman wanted to have it pried out to add to his museum of curiosities, but Phil Jullien handed him one out of his pocket and told him to take it along and say it was the last spike as it would do just as well, and you can see it to-day in Mr. Heyman's bar.

Speeches eulogistic of the occasion were made by several gentlemen and then the train was boarded for home. The journey back was uneventful and all arrived in safety at the starting point, happy in having been present at so great a work.

by C.L. Haig

NORTHERN PACIFIC AND MONTANA RAILROAD CO.

ENGINEER'S OFFICE

Homestake MONTANA, *May 12th* 1890

CHIEF ENGINEER'S OFFICE
N. P. & M.
MAY 14, 1890
RAILROAD
HELENA, M.T.

E. H. M. McHenry
Div. Engr.
Dr Sir:

For The Past week work has made some progress on the G-B line but not as much as should have been done with proper forces and tools. At Whitehall all sidetracks have been laid and ballasted and some back work on track in the vicinity fixed up. There has been a small force at work finishing up the bridges and cattle guards east of Pipestone but there still remains some work of this nature to be done.

The force working at completing and jacking up bridges on the East Mountain section has been decreased one crew having been sent to the Red Bluff line. We have had some trouble with one or two bridges settling badly since you were over the line and they have been repaired to some extent. There is still much to do in this line and it will keep a small crew busy for some time.

On the west side a work train was engaged all week in removing slides and loose rock and boulders and Mr. Keefe has devoted his time to this work. The wet weather has caused a resumption of slides in some cuts and there is yet much to do. I have had a deep surface ditch dug on the up hill side of the old tank cut and at present the spring water is running through it instead of into the cut.

The derrick car was rec'd after some delay but it came to us in poor condition for work. I have had to fix it up and will really not get started with it until tomorrow. A start was made at laying additional tracks in the Butte yard, some frogs and switches having been put in and about 1500 feet of the main freight track laid. Ten cars of ties have been loaded at Spire Rock and sent into Butte. The ditch at Spire Rock has not made much progress, the [Italians] being poorly equipped with tools and explosives. I have had to furnish a Blacksmith for them. This work is supposed to be looked after by Pennycook but he has been absent for four or five days. The track force on east end is now at Logan and started on the yard this morning. Gregory is putting in the waterpipes at Whitehall.

On the Red Bluff and Pony lines grading is still in progress at Pony and Norris and will probably be finished this month. On the Red Bluff line up to Saturday night 15 miles of main track had been laid (to Norwegian Gulch) there being no increase during the week. All the sidetracks at Harrison are now in.

Yours truly,
J. C. Patterson
Asst. Engr.

NORTHERN PACIFIC AND MONTANA RAILROAD CO.

ENGINEER'S OFFICE

CHIEF ENGINEER'S OFFICE
N. P. & M.
MAY 17, 1890
RAILROAD
HELENA, M.T.

............*Homestake*...... MONTANA, *May 15th* 1890

E.H.M. McHenry
Div. Engr.
Dr Sir:-

   I am sorry that you do not look upon the matter of putting section crews at work on the line, in the same light as myself and others. It is not my idea to relieve contractors from any work that they are required to do under the contract. The fact is that no matter how well track may be surfaced it will not remain in good condition under traffic without work being done upon it. There are low spots today some of which have been raised by the contractors three times. Take the bad places between Whitehall and Jefferson Id. which have been fixed within ten days and they are getting bad again. Do you think I can succeed in getting contractors to send men from Logan or Butte to repair these places. You have tried to have them do work of this nature, Mr. Kendrick has tried, I have done the same but I fail to remember of ever meeting with any degree of success.. Retaining contractors estimate will not put the line in first class condition by June 1st and supposing I can not get them to do this work, how can we get it in shape. I expect it would take a week or ten days to get section crews on the line. I spoke to Mr. Mills about it this morning and he thought it would be a good plan, to get the crews organized, sections established etc. and have everything ready for the first train.

   I shall not be satisfied about this matter until I hear from you that Mr. Kendrick or the Apr. Officials decline to take hold of it.

          Yours truly,
          J.C. Patterson
          Asst. Engr.

F. 255.   12-3-89. 25M. P

Northern Pacific Railroad

OFFICE MEMORANDUM

To *E.H. McHenry, Eng.*   *Homestake*   *5/22*   18.*90*

     Div. Engr.

Dear Sir:-

   No time card has been made for trains between Logan & Butte. The enclosed is copy of schedule between Logan & Whitehall, the same train runs as an extra between Whitehall & Butte, leaving Butte generally at 6.30 am & arriving at Butte about 7.30 pm.

please find enclosed
corrected list of stations
& distances

       Yours Truly
       J.C. Patterson
       Asst. Engr.

NORTHERN PACIFIC AND MONTANA RAILROAD CO.

ENGINEER'S OFFICE

Homestake MONTANA, *May 22* 1890

E. H. McHenry Esq.
Div. Eng. Helena
Dear Sir,

The following is a list of the stations as now established on the ground together with their distances –

From center of		to	center of
Logan Depot	1079.93 miles		St. Paul
Logan Junction	0.14 "		Logan Depot
Three Forks Depot	5.14 "		H.B. of Logan Junction
Willow Creek Platform	12.21 "		" " "
Sappington Depot	19.03 "		" " "
Jefferson Bar Platform	25.86 "		" " "
Jefferson Isl. Siding	31.01 "		" " "
Whitehall Depot	38.10 "		" " "
Pipestone Springs Siding	44.92 "		" " "
Spire Rock Tank	51.07 "		" " "
Beef Straight Spur	53.46 "		" " "
Lewis Spur H.B.	58.87 "		" " "
Homestake	60.44 "		" " "
West Tunnel Siding	60.84 "		" " "
East Butte	68.06 "		" " "
Montana Union Transfer	68.94 "		" " "
Butte City –	70.51 "		" " "

CHIEF ENGINEER'S OFFICE
N. P. & M.
MAY 24, 1890
RAILROAD
HELENA, M.T.

F. C. Patterson
Asst. Engr.

I can add but little to the knowledge you gained on your recent visit. The forces were mostly concentrated at the Butte and Logan yards, considerable work being done at Butte. Work on the ditch at Spire Rock [to supply water to the tank] has been somewhat interrupted by crews being taken to load ties. About 2000 feet of ditch is completed to date. Platforms have been built at Jefferson Bar and Willow Creek and some other work done on buildings at Logan. Water pipe is laid at Whitehall and Logan. Work is still in progress on the bridges.

As the work dragged on, Keefe and Green submitted requests for additional compensation. This put Kendrick and McHenry in a bit of a dilemma. They did not believe the contractors deserved more, but on the other hand they did not want to alienate Keefe & Green's influential bondsmen Hammond and Bonner.

In May Kendrick attempted to resolve the matter by putting forward a "final" $50,000 payment offer to Keefe and Green. He sent the following directive to McHenry,

I send you herewith a voucher for $50,000 in favor of Green & Keefe, together with a copy of stipulation, which is drawn in exact accordance with the understanding, and which is to be signed by William H. Green, Michael H. Keefe, Andrew B. Hammond, and Edward L. Bonner. The signatures should be witnessed by two people. Have this document properly exceucted before parting with the voucher.

This failed to satisfy the contractors, however. They rejected the offer and threatened lawsuit. Kendrick and the board of directors refused to budge and turned the matter over to the legal department.

While negotiations over payment continued, work on the ground progressed. Crews finished the ditch at Spire Rock and waited for the 7,600 feet of pipe. Other crews removed boulders that continued to fall into the cuts, and bridge crews strove to raise bridges -- some of which were as far as six inches out of alignment. Even the 1895 timetable shows a ten mile per hour speed restric-

This 1997 photo shows the ditch referred to by J.C. Patterson in his letter to E.H. McHenry on May 21st. This ditch ultimately would be over 7,600 feet long bringing water from Halfway Creek to below the tank. Presumably a pump below the bridge pumped water to the tank. Evidence on the ground indicates the ditch was abandoned soon after construction although the Spire Rock tank survived until the 20's.

Northern Pacific papers, K. Ross Toole Archives, The University of Montana

8 1-90, 2M. S   C.D. 66.

Northern Pacific Railroad Company

Construction Department

PERSONAL   St. Paul, Minn., October 11, 1890

E.H. McHenry, Esq.,
    Principal Assistant Engineer.

Dear Sir:-
    The Assistant Treasurer notified me yesterday, that Green & Keefe, through their assignee, Harvey Barbour, had declined to accept vouchers for final payment on account of the Gallatin-Butte and Red Bluff contracts. I wired this to Mr. Oakes, and told him that I thought this would bring the matter to a head, with a possibility that the contractors would commence suit, as they have many times threatened to do. I received the following message from Mr. Oakes this morning:
    "We will now stand on the letter of our contract, in dealing with Green & Keefe.
    If they bring suit, we must put in counter claim for damages by delay and otherwise."
    It will be necessary to exercise a great deal of care not to commit ourselves or the Company to any arrangement for a settlement, or at least to make any proposition, directly or indirectly, for the payment of any additional sums upon these contracts. We should be very glad to avoid the process of long litigation, in the settlement of this matter, but it seems to me, as it does to Mr. Oakes, that considering the loss that the Company has sustained, by reason of the utter failure of the contractors to comply with the requirements of the contract, with respect to the proper supervision and energetic prosecution of the work, more than offsets any claims that they have made for additional compensation. I shall particularly regret the necessity for a suit, which will inevitably place the bondsmen, Messrs. Bonner & Hammond, in the position of defendants, as our relations with these gentlemen have been uniformly pleasant. They will undoubtedly recognize our position; and Mr. Bonner must clearly understand, and indeed has so expressed himself, both to you and to me, that the contractors utterly failed to give the work proper attention, and that it is necessary for the Company to take measures to protect itself from further loss.
    You should at once get your records into such shape that we can file an answer in any suit that may be brought by Green & Keefe; and also be able to draw a full and comprehensive complaint in the suit, which we must, in this case, bring against them.

Yours, very truly,

J.W. Kendrick

Chief Engineer

tion over all bridges on the mountain.

In Butte tracks for the yard at the Montana Union transfer were laid, and the ground preparation was finished for the new depot which was to be one block east of Main Street on Mercury. The NP had taken offense to the siting of the MC depot in Helena which was at the end of a long stub right in the heart of Last Chance Gulch, and it had decided to locate its depot in Butte closer to the downtown district than the MC depot. Economy prevailed, however, and the depot was never built. The NP continued to use the MU depot until they acquired the MU yard in 1898 and built the present brick depot in 1905.

J.D. Finn, project engineer for the Elkhorn branch, surveyed the BSL on June 7th and reported to G.W. Dickinson, the Asst. General Superintendent in Helena, that he found "the main line in fairly good condition and surfaced." He stated that crews were making progress changing out 56 pound frogs for the required 66 pound frogs, and,

> If we take hold of this branch June 15th, we will have considerable work to do which should have been done by the Construction Department, and I think they should be made to pay the expense of doing the same during the latter part of June and all of July.

In Butte the company was having problems with people who had filed mining claims when they learned where the company was planning to put their terminal facilities. Many of these claims had been artfully avoided by McHenry when he surveyed the line, but some still remained and needed to be resolved.

The Butte Short Line was formally turned over to the operating department on June 14, 1890, despite its unfinished state.

Excursions & Operations

Two excursions were planned during the summer of 1890 to celebrate the opening of the new line. One was planned for the citizens of Butte to go to Bozeman which was being groomed as the eastern terminus of the line, and a later excursion was planned to bring the people of Bozeman the other way. Considerable planning went into both occasions.

The Butte to Bozeman excursion ran on May 26th. Concerned that no unpleasant events mar the occasion, Kendrick wired McHenry,

> See that we have a thoroughly competent crew to handle the train.... Take every precaution to prevent

---

OPENING A BRANCH LINE

First Excursion Over the Butte-Gallatin Branch of the Northern Pacific

Bozeman does the Agreeable As Host For the Large Party

Bozeman, May 26, -[Special.]- The Butte and Bozeman celebration was one of the greatest days Bozeman has ever seen. The weather was fine and the verdure so far advanced as to make a beautiful picture for the citizens of the mining town. A delegation from the board of trade went to Logan and met the Butte party, which occupied nine coaches and was composed of fully 300 people. The excursionists were provided with music by the Alice band and in charge of Jimmy McCaig. The party were united in praising the road bed of the new road and the grand scenery en route.

Arriving at Bozeman they were welcomed by the local band, the firing of cannons, and a speech from General Wilson.... The farmers who had come from near and far, together with the townspeople, then took the excursionists for a ride around the city, first taking them to the hill east of town where the whole valley in all its loveliness could be seen. The visitors were then taken to the city hall where dinner was spread for them..... At 4 o'clock those who wished to ride were conveyed to the depot, while those who preferred to walk followed the Bozeman band on foot, singing "Marching Through Georgia." At the depot several more speeches were made by Mr. Dolman, Mr. Bray, Mr. Hennessey and others of Butte.

Then, with three cheers for Bozeman, responded to by three cheers for Butte, the merry party pulled out for home, declaring that they had enjoyed their visit immensely. Every store on Main street was decorated with bunting....

Daily Independent   May 27, 1890

---

drinking on the part of your train men during the day.

Kendrick need not have worried, the excursion went off without a hitch. 300 Butte people in nine coaches made the trip. Agent McCaig provided a band from the Alice Mine to entertain, and everyone praised "the condition of the track."

Representatives from the Bozeman Board of Trade met the train at Logan and accompanied the Butte delegation into Bozeman. Speeches were given and tours were taken. The happy group, pledging renewed cooperation between the two cities, returned that night over the newly completed road.

On June 19th the railroad sponsored an excursion in the other direction for citizens of Bozeman to visit Butte. Eight coaches were provided by the railroad for the occasion. The Bozeman delegation sprinkled flowers on the Butte crowd as they entered the city, and they in turn were greeted by a rousing speech from W.A. Clark. The enjoyment was so compelling that the return home did not begin until midnight.

Daily passenger trains began on June 15, 1890. Additional side tracks were installed in Bozeman. A timetable was published and the *Daily Independent* announced on that date, "The trains from and to Butte will arrive and leave here [Garrison] simultaneously, according to the time-table, while there will be twenty minutes difference at Logan." A similar story on June 25th explains the consist of the train,

> The passenger train which leaves Bozeman for Butte consists of baggage car, coach and sleeper. The sleeper is taken from No. 1, passenger, attached here, and runs to Butte and on to Garrison. The same plan is observed at Garrison on the train coming east through Butte. The express matter for Butte is transferred at Bozeman, and the Butte train follows the one going via Helena to Garrison. The time is 9:30 a.m.

N. P. & M. R. R.
CONSTRUCTION DEPARTMENT
GALLATIN -- BUTTE DIVISION

In Effect Feb 1st 1890

west bound   east bound

No. 5	No. 3	No.1 *Leaves Daily*	Distance from Logan	Schedule No. _____ STATIONS	Capacity sidings - cars	No. 2	No. 4	No. 6
		1:00 A.M.	.0	Logan 5.3		11:06 A.M		
		1:27	5.3	Three Forks 13.7		10:45		
		7:15 / 3:15	19.0	Sappington 11.8		9:50 / 8:47		
		4:02	30.8	Jefferson Island 7.3		8:00		
		4:30 A.M.	38.1	Whitehall 6.9		7:30 A.M		
			45.0	Pipestone Springs 8.3				
			53.5	Beef-Straight 6.9				
			60.4	Homestake 8.6				
			69.0	South Butte 1.5				
			70.5	Butte				

East Bound Trains Have Right to Road.
Train no two (2) will not leave _____ until train one (1) arrives.
No train will exceed 18 miles per hour without special orders.

Speed must be reduced to eight (8) miles per hour on all truss bridges.
All concerned will be governed by Northern Pacific Transportation Rules.

W.R. Mansfield, Train Master, SAPPINGTON, MONT.

E.H. McHenry, Division Engineer, HOMESTAKE, MONT.

F.T. Robertson, Res. Engineer, SAPPINGTON, MONT.

Northern Pacific papers, K. Ross Toole Archives, The University of Montana

A temporary timetable for trains operating between Logan and Whitehall was issued Feb 1, 1890, five and one half months before the BSL was turned over to the operating department. The mountain was not open, but traffic was already flowing east.

Butte politics and increasing passenger traffic caused NP officials to reroute Nos. 1 & 2 via Butte entirely, and the first through train stopped at Butte on September 3, 1890. This was temporarily discontinued in 1891, but soon Nos. 1 & 2 returned to the BSL. It became known as the "passenger line," and the Helena route became known as the "freight line." The "Route of the North Coast Limited" became that of the Butte Short Line.

Butte-Gallatin Branch

The citizens of Butte, or at least a portion of them who accepted the hospitalities of the construction department of the NP presented valuable souvenirs to Messrs. McHenry and Patterson, who supervised the construction of the branch, and also to the genial James McCaig, agent of the NP at Butte. The latter gentleman, in the course of a few remarks responsive to the gift tendered to him -- a gold watch -- displayed his loyalty to Butte by saying he expected to see through Northern Pacific trains passing through Butte east and west before long. He but voiced the one wish of west-siders, but acknowledged the NP was not in a position to do this at present on account of having no line out of Butte to the west. There are several reasons to show why Helena will remain on the main line. The distance from St. Paul to either city is just five miles in Butte's favor. The city of Butte is on the same elevation as the much-abused-by-West-siders Mullan tunnel. The Homestake Pass, over which the Butte-Gallatin branch crosses the main divide of the Rockies is 800 feet higher than the Mullan tunnel, and the Homestake pass is 300 feet lower than the Pipestone....

Daily Independent   **May 30, 1890**

THE FIRST THROUGH TRAIN

The Northern Pacific Flyer Reaches Butte Promptly on Schedule Time

A Splendidly Equipped Train -- The Passengers Wanted to Know All About Butte

The first through train over the Northern Pacific via the new route from Garrison through Butte to Logan, passed through the city yesterday afternoon at 3:25. The train was composed of a baggage, mail and express cars and five coaches heavily laden with through passengers: also a dining car and a Pullman sleeper. The coaches, diner and sleeper, ever the essence of elegance, being elaborately finished in mahogany and polished cherry, between the panels of which were beveled-edged French plate glass mirrors. The train pulled up to the depot on the dot, having made a rapid and successful run from Garrison.

Through the courtesy of General Agent McCaig, a number of reporters, representing the journals of Butte, were accorded the pleasure of a trip to Pipestone on the train, which was pulled by engine 441, with engineer George Howe at the throttle. Conductor Cunningham had charge of the train, while Brakemen Jones and Babcock performed the necessary wheel polishing, but as the train, like all others, was equipped with air brakes, the duties of Babcock and Jones in this particular are not calculated to callous their hands or break their backs.

Leaving Butte the train was pulled by a "double header," that is two engines, both of which were of the straight stack and extension front pattern. Passing around the horseshoe above Meaderville, the ascent of the grade to Pipestone pass [Homestake] began, and the sharp, heavy exhaust of the engines indicated that they had gotten down to solid work. The grim mountains, rising a thousand feet above the train on one side, with the broad expanse of sunlit valley, dotted over with ranches, smiling on the other, presented a scene which the passengers highly enjoyed. All of them had heard of Butte, but few of them had ever seen the city before. The great majority of the passengers were far eastern people, returning from a visit to the coast.....

The west-bound train arrived last night at 2:35. A baggage, mail and express car, four coaches and two sleepers made up the train. The run from Logan to Butte was made on time with ease, and Garrison was doubtless reached on the dot, as the Montana Union roadbed is solid and ironed with the best sixty-pound steel. The service is all that could be desired, and the new route is destined to become most desireable and popular with the traveling public.

Superintendent Dickinson, who accompanied the train from Garrison to Butte, was well pleased at the new departure and was the recipient of warm congratulations for the material assistance he had rendered in securing for Butte the valuable service of the through trains.

Butte Miner   **Sept. 4, 1890**

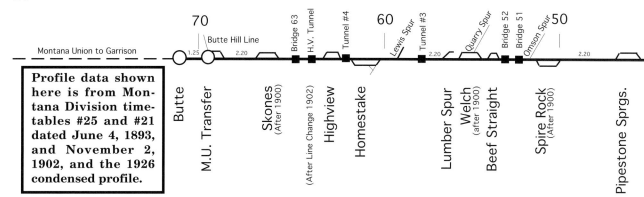

Profile data shown here is from Montana Division timetables #25 and #21 dated June 4, 1893, and November 2, 1902, and the 1926 condensed profile.

Montana Union to Garrison

70   Butte Hill Line   Bridge 63   H.V. Tunnel   Tunnel #4   60   Lewis Spur   Tunnel #3   Quarry Spur   Bridge 52   Bridge 51   Omson Spur   50

Butte · M.U. Transfer · Skones (After 1900) · (After Line Change 1902) · Highview · Homestake · Lumber Spur · Welch (after 1900) · Beef Straight · Spire Rock (After 1900) · Pipestone Sprgs.

3. Aboard Train #13

According to the 1902 employee timetable there were three passenger trains and two scheduled freights operating over the Butte Short Line each day. Let us step back to 1902 and board west bound train #13, the local passenger connection at Logan, and ride to Butte. We leave Logan at 8:05 AM and arrive in Butte at 10:58 AM with three scheduled stops.

The first is a station stop at Whitehall, the second for water at Spire Rock or Homestake and the third is for a meet with #34 at Welch.

The sun has just risen over the Bridger Mountains to the east as we climb up the steps of our coach. The conductor punches our tickets and announces we will be leaving shortly. The engineer blows the whistle, and we depart Logan on time.

As #13 gains speed we gradually descend to the Madison River crossing at bridge #4. This is one of the three rivers which come together to form the Missouri two miles to the northwest.

The first station is Three Forks at mile post 5. There is nothing here really except the depot. At one time Marcus Daly, the Butte copper magnate, planned to build a smelter here, but he chose to erect it in Great Falls instead. In another six years the Milwaukee will utilize Three Forks as a division point.

After clearing the siding, the engineer throttles out once again for Willow Creek five miles away. The train is on straight track on a gentle upgrade, so it is making good speed. We are in a broad valley with the Jefferson River in view to the right and a high, bench land to the left.

We pass through Willow Creek at 8:25. The tracks are now along the south bank of the Jefferson River, and the valley tightens as we pass what will be known later as Ingleside Spur. At 8:27 the train arrives at Sappington Jct. (mile post 19). Sappington is where the Red Bluff and Pony line branches off to the south. This branch was built by the same contractors who built the BSL, and it serves the mining

The west bound NCL near Lime Spur at about mile post 28 in the late 1920's.   **JVM**

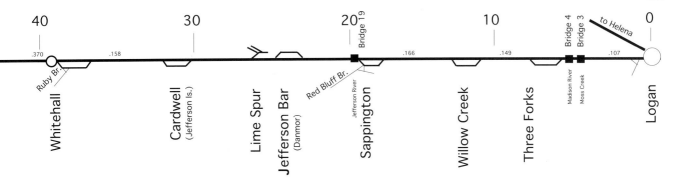

district at Pony as well as agricultural shippers at Harrison and Norris with stage connections to the Madison Valley and Yellowstone Park. Train #33, the local mixed train, has just left Norris and will be following us to Butte two hours later.

Immediately after leaving Sappington, we cross the Jefferson River at Bridge 19 and enter the rugged part of the Jefferson Canyon. Shear limestone cliffs rise up on both sides of the train. The roadbed is carved out of the rock right along the river's edge. It is obvious the river has made this valley by forcing its way through a seam in the limestone.

Train #13 passes the old siding of Jefferson Bar (later Danmor). Water percolating through the limestone has created Morrison's Cave (Lewis & Clark Caverns) in the cliffs above us to the north, but this is not a stop for us. Oldtimers tell of armed conflicts between surveying crews of the Union Pacific and Northern Pacific over rights-of-way through here in the 1880's.

At mile post 27 the train passes Lime Spur and its small yard where ore hoppers wait for the local freight. Lime is mined here for flux in the smelters at Butte and Anaconda. If a blast is imminent, #13 may have to wait until the track is cleared. Later, signals will be placed here to protect this section of track.

At 8:57 we leave the narrow canyon and steam through Jeff-erson Island siding. The valley broadens out before the river turns south towards Dillon. This station will be renamed Cardwell after the Milwaukee Road builds through the canyon.

The first scheduled stop for train #13 is Whitehall at mile post 38, and we arrive at 9:10. The grade from Logan to Whitehall has been at water level rising at a rate of less than 1 %. With the exception of a few tight corners in Jefferson Canyon, the track has been fast with gentle curves. Just past Whitehall everything changes. The mountain district begins here as the track leaves the Jefferson River and follows Big Pipestone Creek and later Homestake Creek toward the divide.

Whitehall also serves as the junction with the Gaylord and Ruby Valley which has just been extended to Alder. The local, #44, will depart at 2:20 and is making up in the yard. There are a four stall roundhouse, coal and water facilities and a new, single story depot. The town sits north of the tracks across a large, grassy park. At Whitehall heavier trains pick up helper locomotives, and a 2-8-0 stands ready at the coal dock to push.

A short run up Big Pipestone Creek west from Whitehall brings us to the beginning of the 15 miles of 2.2% grade leading to the summit of the continental divide at Homestake Pass.

We barely start to climb on the steep grade when the train passes Pipestone Springs at mile post 45. Across the creek to the south is a sprawling resort featuring a natural hot springs. An excursion train, which has brought people from the smokey environments of Butte and Anaconda for a day's outing in the fresh air, sits on the siding.

A 1920's view of the rocks below Highview taken from the platform of an observation car.   JVM

From NP Timetable #21 for the Montana Division, issued SUNDAY, NOVEMBER 2nd, 1902

West Bound								BUTTE LINE						East Bound	
FREIGHT No.55	FREIGHT No.33	PASSENG'R No.13	PASSENG'R No.5	PASSENG'R No.1	Water, Coal, Stock Tables and Wyes	Station Numbers	Distance from Logan	Time Table No. 21 Nov. 2d, 1902 Succeeding No. 20A	Distance from Garrison	Capacity of Passing Tracks	PASSENG'R No.2	PASSENG'R No.6	PASSENG'R No.14	FREIGHT No.34	FREIGHT No.56
S'nd Cl's	S'nd Cl's	First Class	First Class	First Class				STATIONS			First Class	First Class	First Class	S'nd Cl's	S'nd Cl's
DAILY	EX.SUNDAY	DAILY	DAILY	DAILY				Tel. Offices & Calls			DAILY	DAILY	DAILY	EX.SUNDAY	DAILY
De 3.45 AM M 56		De 8.05 AM	De 10.30 AM	De 3.45 PM M14	WC STY	1120	0.0	Logan CH 5.5 N	121.9	60	See P'ge 2 Ar 3.45 AM M55	See Page 2 Ar.2.30 AM	Ar 3.15 PM M1		Ar 3.35 AM See Pg2 M55
4.05		* 8.15	F 10.40	* 3.54		TD 5	5.5	Three Forks 6.9	116.4	70	* 3.33	* 2.15	F 3.00		3.05
4.30		* 8.25	F 10.50	* 4.04		TD 13	12.4	Willow Creek 6.8	109.5	70	* 3.23	* 2.05	F 2.49	See 34 R.B.& P.Bh Pg 6	2.40
4.55	De 11.10 AM C5	* 8.37	F 11.02 C33	* 4.13	WCY	TD 19	19.2	Sappington SO 7.7 N	102.7	70	* 3.12	F 1.52	2.38 C34	Ar 2.00 PM C14	2.20
5.25	11.40	* 8.50	F 11.15	* 4.25		TD 27	26.9	Lime Spur 4.4	95.0		* 3.00	* 1.40	F 2.25	1.25	1.40
5.45	11.59 AM	* 8.57	F 11.23	* 4.32		TD 31	31.3	Jefferson Is'd 7.0	90.6	75	* 2.50	* 1.30 P 56	F 2.18	1.00	De 1.35 6P Ar 1.25
Ar 6.15 De 6.45	Ar 12.30 P M34 De 1.15	9.10	11.40 M34	4.50	WCY	TD 38	38.3	Whitehall WH 6.8 N	83.6	40	2.40	1.20	2.08	De 12.50 PM Ar 11.35 M33	12.45
7.15	Ar 1.50 De 1.55 M14	* 9.25	11.55 AM	* 5.06		TD 45	45.1	Pipestone 4.9	76.8	75	* 1.05	* 1.05 M33	1.55 M33	11.05	12.20
7.50	2.35	* 9.45	* 12.15 PM	* 5.27	W 1 3/4 miles W	TD 50	50.0	Spire Rock 3.7	71.9	65	* 2.10	* 12.50	* 1.40	10.40	12.05 AM
8.20	3.05	* 10.05	* 12.35	* 5.47		TD 54	53.7	Beef Straight 1.0	68.2	12	* 1.59	* 12.38	* 1.29	10.15	11.50 PM
8.30	3.15	* 10.08 M 34	F 12.40	* 5.51		TD 55	54.7	Welch H 4.4 D	67.2	65	* 1.56	* 12.36	F 1.26	De 10.08 M13 Ar 10.03	11.45
9.15	3.50	* 10.25	* 12.59	* 6.10		TD 59	59.1	Lewis Spur 1.6	62.8		* 1.44	* 12.24	* 1.14	9.40	11.30
9.30 M34	4.05	* 10.33	F 1.10 M14	* 6.18	W	TD 60	60.7	Homestake HO 0.4 N	61.2	75	* 1.40	* 12.20	* 1.10 M 5	9.30 M55	11.20
9.35	4.10	* 10.35	* 1.15	* 6.23		TD 61	61.1	Highview 8.1	60.8	22	* 1.35	* 12.15	* 1.05	9.25	11.15
10.30 C 13	4.50	* 10.58 C 55	* 1.40	* 6.50		TD 70	69.2	M.U. Transfer 1.5	52.7	40	* 1.00	* 11.45	* 12.38	10.10	10.10
Ar 10.45 AM Daily	Ar 5.00 PM Ex Sun				S	TD 71	BY Butte D 6.8 (N.P. Depot)	51.2						De 8.15 AM Ex Sun	De 10.00 PM Daily
		Ar 11.05 AM Daily D 2.00	Ar 1.50 M 8 D 2.00	Ar 7.00 De 7.10	West Y	U O	70.7	W Butte N 6.8 (M.U.Depot)	51.2	300	De 12.50 Ar 12.40	De 11.35 Ar 11.25	De 12.30 PM Daily		

Registering stations - Logan, Whitehall, M.U. Transfer, N.P. Depot Butte.
Bulletin stations - Logan, M.U. Transfer, Butte.
Time clocks - Livingston, Butte.
Mountain grades from two miles east of Pipestone to two miles east of M.U. Transfer
55 and 56 will not carry passengers except by special permission from Superintendent.

Switches at Logan will be kept locked for N.P. main track. Switches at Sappington will be kept locked for Butte Line main track.
On Mountain grades ascending freight trains will take siding when meeting other trains and ascending passenger trains will take siding when meeting passenger trains.

Black smoke pours from the stack of #13's locomotive as the engineer throttles out for more power. Almost immediately the train enters a series of eight to twelve degree curves as the railroad trades distance for elevation on three looping curves between Pipestone and Spire Rock sidings.

The country also changes. What has been largely a trip along the river and creek bottoms, lined with cottonwoods, is now a trip through large granite boulders and sagebrush. The country is arid, but the scenery is spectacular. The snow capped Tobacco Root Mountains are off to the south beyond the Jefferson Valley, and the continental divide looms above us. To the north we can see a granite outcrop rising two hundred feet above the surrounding country. This feature is named Spire Rock and remains a landmark as long as we are on the east side of the pass. It also is the namesake for the next station.

As #13 approaches the new siding at Spire Rock (mile post 50), passengers can look out the left side windows and see the track across the canyon and above them at Welch (mile post 55) -- only a mile away as the crow flies. Now the train begins an eight mile-long loop around the Big Pipestone Creek drainage to gain elevation. Spire Rock siding at 5,224 feet above sea level is almost 500 feet lower than Welch just across the rugged, boulder-strewn valley.

Without stopping at Spire Rock siding, we continue our journey into the loop. Almost immediately we pass Omsun's Spur. Two stock cars are spotted here at the loading chute. Two more tight curves and the locomotive stops at Spire Rock tank.

A wooden tank serves water hungry locomotives working the east side. A section house and pump station sit along the side of the tracks. Several houses are just over the ridge. We get off briefly to take in the spectacular scenery around us.

The engine stands on the approach to the new 13 span, 520 foot long Spire Rock Viaduct (bridge 51). Originally wooden, this bridge is one of those which held up the opening of the line in 1890. Just a year ago the bridge was rebuilt of steel as part of a general upgrade of the line.

The creek below us is Halfway Creek, a small stream showing signs of placer mining. A mile and a half long flume brings water to the pump. All around us are granite upthrusts, the biggest of which is Spire Rock which dominates the skyline to the northwest. After the engine waters, the engineer blows his whistle, and we all scurry aboard. At 9:45 the journey resumes.

In just a bit over a mile, but after several narrow cuts in the granite and some tight curves, the train passes over another steel trestle. This is Big Pipestone Creek Bridge (bridge 52), an 11 span, 360 foot structure. Like bridge 51 it was originally wooden and has just been rebuilt of steel. The train is now at the head of the loop, the west end of the bridge actually begins the curve to the south as the road climbs towards Beef Straight and Welch. The scenery is now tight around the train, but it is far more wooded than below. Pine and Douglas fir with an occasional grove of mountain aspen have replaced the arid sagebrush. After passing through a long narrow cut the tracks break out into a grass covered park near mile post 54.

Now the train passes Beef Straight siding which is being replaced by Welch siding with its new telegraph station a mile beyond. The only facilities at Beef Straight are for the loading of livestock. It soon will be abandoned.

Beyond mile post 54 we cross old bridge 54 which is in the process of being filled in. It was here that the two segments of the Butte Short Line were joined in a ceremony March 29, 1890. The celebrated "last spike" is supposedly on display in a bar in Butte.

At 10:08 train #13 arrives at the new Welch telegraph station where the order board in front of the small depot signals it to stop. We have a scheduled meet here with #34, the west bound freight working from Butte to Logan. As we wait, the operator hands up orders to the engine crew on the locomotive, and the conductor steps down to sign for his. The operator has been able to watch our train ascend ever since it left Whitehall from his vantage point in the small telegraph station.

Within two minutes #34 drifts by us on the siding. The smell of hot iron permeates the coach. The retainers and wheels on the passing train are hot from descending the steep grade.

Just below Welch is the beginning of a spur reaching up Beef Straight Creek to a quarry where granite is mined for many of the buildings in Butte. The Federal Court House, the base for the Daly statue and the high school are good examples. There is a small community of quarry workers here, and at times locomotive #102 can be seen bringing down six or seven flat cars with dressed stone blocks aboard for pick up by #33, the west bound freight.

Our engine whistles, and we start out again. Above Welch the

A Butte Hill Mystery

This photo, taken from the 1902 *Wonderland* is captioned "Rock spire on the Butte Air Line," and it is something of a mystery. Most likely the photo was taken by F.J. Haynes during one of his trips over the BSL in the 1890's although the plate is not in his collection at the Montana Historical Society. It was the authors' intention to duplicate this photo since this type of rock formation is unique to Homestake Pass. Despite numerous trips to the area, however, we could not find the spire. There are several similar spires, but none are this one. Have trees grown up and obscured it? Is it farther from the grade than first thought? Did the freeway take it out during construction? Were we just not able to see it? We do not have an answer.

country changes once more. It is now more open with groves of alder and pine surrounding open parks. Behind us we can see Pipestone Rock looming over Welch Quarry. Four years from now a dramatic holdup attempt will be made here, and the engineer on the east bound Burlington Flyer will be shot and killed. At mile

post 56 we pass the site of Lumber Spur which has now been removed.

Below us, we can see Spire Rock siding and the dramatic country in between, littered with gigantic boulders and volcanic upthrusts simlar to the granite tower pictured in the 1902 *Wonderland*. We soon turn due west and follow another mountain valley toward the summit. Large rocks still abound, and near mile post 57 we pass through a short 117 foot long tunnel carved through the living rock. In the 1920's locomotive 2120 will go over the bank here when it strikes a rock.

It is just three miles now to the summit, but the locomotive still has to work hard on the steep grade. We pass a small pond on the right with the dubious name of Isa Lake. At mile post 59 we pass Lewis Spur, the site of a tie camp belonging to a Butte alderman.

Just a mile later we cross the east switch of Homstake siding. A spur enters a pit which provides most of the decomposed granite fill the company uses on the line. A steam shovel and a string of hoppers can be seen in the pit.

At 10:33 our train arrives at Homestake station, the 6,328 foot summit of the pass. Helpers are turned on the 60 foot turntable. A section house and several shacks accomodate the railroad personnel who live here. A small depot serves as a telegraph station, and a water tank is near by.

Our train slows as it enters the 706 foot long tunnel. The crew sets the retainers as we top the hill at the east portal. We immediately begin our decent down the 2.2% grade to Butte only ten miles away.

At the west end of the tunnel, the train passes Highview siding which is now largely unused. It was here that the original line went out around a ridge and across a timber trestle. We can still see the original cut through the rocky ridge, but in 1901 a new 628 foot tunnel was bored at mile post 62 which eased the curvature considerably. The line is still dramatic as the train loops around huge granite boulders and into timber-lined Highview Tunnel, tunnel #5.

After the tunnel the passengers on the left side of the train get their first view of Silver Bow Valley below them. The view is incredible as the track clings to the mountainside as it descends from the summit. The curves are still tight, and we pass over several wooden trestles that have recently been filled in with dirt and rock. This was the most difficult part of the line to construct in 1889, and over 1,000 laborers worked to blast out the roadbed.

Train #13 passes over bridge 63, a 13 span, 530 foot long, steel bridge over Ealean Gulch. The bridge is on a 12 degree curve, and

the passengers exclaim as the super elevation of the curve makes the coach seem to lurch out over the dry gulch.

Near mile post 65 the train passes construction equipment in the process of building the new siding of Skones (initially Adams). Skones siding will wrap around the last 12 degree curve on the decent to Butte, and it is near here that the Italian laborers' camp was burned by the sheriff during the construction in 1889.

As the train rounds the corner at mile post 66, we get a magnificent view of Butte, "the Richest Hill on Earth." It is now only four miles away, and the mining district and the smoke from the smelters are clearly visible. Next year there will be a succesful robbery here, and the robbers will escape back into Butte with their loot. The engineer on the train will be Frank Clow, the same man who

will be killed in the 1907 hold up attempt at Welch.

We come down the last bit of grade, cross Silver Bow Creek on an impressive wooden trestle and arrive at the Montana Union Transfer at 10:58 AM -- exactly on time. The train slows as it makes its way through the switches. Our destination is the depot at the former Montana Union yard.

We come to a stop at the station. The NP is still using the Montana Union depot. The impressive, two story brick NP building will not be finished for three more years. It will be built near this site. Northern Pacific passengers always did arrive here, and the station has been operated by the NP since 1898. The Union Pacific shares the facility. At one time there were plans to build a station closer to downtown, but they never bore fruit. The old NP

This 1910 postcard view of the new brick depot in Butte, Montana, shows what a busy place it was. It was completed in 1905 on the site of the old Montana Union depot after the demise of that road. The NP's Butte depot had previously been several blocks to the north on Arizona Street near the original freight yard.

067 — NORTHERN PACIFIC DEPOT, BUTTE, MONTANA.

The 1897 "Bird's Eye View of Butte" taken from *Across the Continent Via the Northern Pacific* published by A.C. Riley shows the Montana Union depot and yards in its lower right corner.

freight yard is farther up the hill and a bit to the east from here. Baggage wagons, porters and the friends and relatives meeting #13's passengers fill the platform in front of the depot. As we climb from our coach and move through the waiting room to the street, we are greeted by horse-drawn cabs, a sophisticated street railway system and advertisements for Butte's finest hotels.

We can only marvel at the magnificent journey we have had and the wonderful scenery we have seen the last three hours as we rode #13 over the Butte Short Line.

Car #2 of Butte's Metropolitan Electric Railway carries a load of young people and their bicycles to the "South Butte Depot" in 1890 or 1891. Incorporated May 23, 1890, the line merged with the other streetcar operations in Butte a year later to become the Butte Consolidated Railway Company. In 1899 it became the Butte Electric Railway Company which operated until September 22, 1937. In 1890 South Butte Depot would be the Montana Union depot which also served NP and UP passengers. The BER also hauled ore from the mines to transfer facilities at the various rail yards. WMM

4. The River Line: Logan to Whitehall

Logan:

This 1911 view is taken from the cliffs across the Gallatin River. It shows early Logan and the railroad installations there. The BSL leaves the main line at the far end of the yard.

The Butte Short Line tracks begin at Logan, originally known as Canyon House. Facilities at Logan were primitive at first. In the early years a small station and water tank made up the railroad installations. The town hosted a couple of saloons, a rudimentary hotel and a general store.

Initially Bozeman was viewed by the Northern Pacific as the eastern terminus of the Butte Short Line, and the company installed a roundhouse, engine ser-

vice and yard tracks. In 1895 similar facilities were built at Logan to save the 28 miles operating distance. The citizens of Bozeman vigorously protested the change. They even sent a delegation to St. Paul, but it was to no avail. The BSL became part of the Montana Division of the NP and was dispatched out of Livingston.

Near Logan the tracks of the BSL cross the Madison River at a point only three miles above the Three Forks of the Missouri. The

main line follows the Missouri to Helena after crossing the Gallatin at Logan.

In later years a brick depot was built at Logan, and Helena passengers wishing to travel on the North Coast Limited were bussed to and from Logan to meet the trains. Secondary trains provided passenger service directly to Helena and other points on the "freight line" after 1892. The BSL became known as the "passenger line."

A sketch by Lanser depicting the confluence of the Gallatin, Madison and the Jefferson Rivers at the Three Forks of the Missouri appears in the 1886-7 *Northern Pacific Guide*. The artist was on the hill above Trident. The view is up the valley of the Jefferson along the route of what would become the Butte Short Line. Logan, or Canyon House as it was known then, is just out of the view to the left.

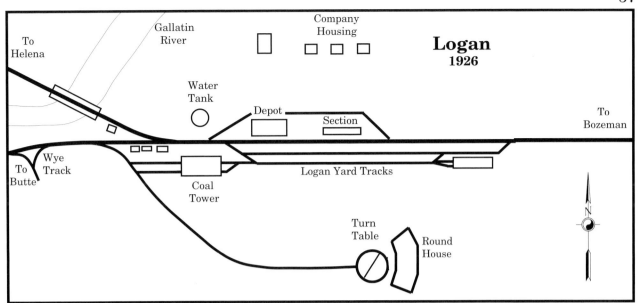

At Logan the Butte Short Line leaves the main line. Originally it was known as Canyon House. In later years a brick depot, coal tower and extended yard facilities could be found here. A double track main east of Logan was built to Livingston.

This 1920's view looks down the Gallatin River at the west switch of Logan Yard. The wye track leads are to the left. The Milwaukee branch line overpass can be seen in the distance as it crosses over the BSL on its way to Bozeman. The road bridge provides access to farms across the river. The Helena main line is just out of the picture to the right. Three Forks is five miles to the west.

B2183 Gallatin Bridge, Logan, Mont.

DISASTROUS FIRE VISITS LOGAN - TWO MEN ALMOST SUFFOCATED

Bozeman, Feb. 20 - Logan, the junction of the Butte and Helena branches of the Northern Pacific railroad, was visited by a disastrous fire last night. Some half dozen or more buildings were burned to the ground, the loss being estimated at $6,000 with but little insurance. Albert Freak and Frank Evans, while trying to save one of the buildings, were nearly suffocated. Evans is now in a precarious condition.

The fire started about 9 o'clock in a store building occupied by Mr. Maezcher and was supposed to have been caused by a defective flue which set fire to the attic.

Before the flames were extinguished buildings occupied by G. Bertelsen, a Chinese laundry, Maezcher's store, Gilhery's restaurant, several outbuildings were destroyed. Only through the hard work on the part of the citizens, the Hutchinson building and a string of houses on the east of Roland's store were saved and it was while working in the Hutchinson building that Freak and Evans were nearly suffocated. They had been putting wet blankets on the roof when a sudden puff of wind sent the flames and smoke in their direction.

The Northern Pacific railway company sent to Bozeman fire department asking for aid, as its roundhouse and other buildings were in danger. Mayor Morris permitted the fire engine and several hundred feet of hose to go, and they were taken over on a flat car with a special engine.

Missoulian   **February 21, 1903**

Three Forks:

Three Forks at mile post 7 was never a large station on the BSL. It was far more important to the Milwaukee which established a division point there. The town grew around the Milwaukee rather than the NP.

Three Forks takes its name from the confluence of three rivers which combine five miles north of the town to form the Missouri River. Captain Lewis of the Lewis & Clark Expedition named the three rivers the Gallatin (for the Secretary of the Treasury), the Madison (for the Secretary of State) and the Jefferson (for the President). A fur trading post and the original town site were located near the headwaters, but Three Forks later was moved up the Jefferson. Until the 1850's,

this was the heartland of the fierce Blackfeet Indians.

Small scale mining took place around Three Forks in the 1880's, but the bigger strikes were farther south near Pony. At one time, however, a huge flume was constructed to carry water to hydraulic mining claims in the valley. Later the Jefferson River near the town site was mined by the largest mechanical dredge of that time.

Just prior to the construction of the Butte Short Line, Marcus Daly bought a great deal of land around Three Forks. Speculation ran rampant that he would locate a smelter there. The volume of water flowing in the Jefferson was found to be less than that in the Missouri at Great Falls, however, and he decided to locate his

smelter in Great Falls instead. Daly's Three Forks land was sold.

Until 1909 Northern Pacific railroad structures at Three Forks must have been quite primitive. On April 15, of that year the *Three Forks Herald* announced,

Sometime ago the Northern Pacific placed a couple of boxcars at their siding near this city to serve as temporary waiting rooms and store houses until more permanent structures could be built. The railroad has just announced they will finally build the depot.

Since the Milwaukee was currently building a roundhouse, creamery, commissary, hospital, stock yard, extensive yards and a large depot, this announcement must have struck the locals as somewhat anticlimactic.

The telegrahic train order at right directs Engineer Carson to run extra from Whitehall to Logan at a speed of 20 miles per hour. The order was issued May 31, 1892, from the superintendent's office in Livingston. High water on the Jefferson or track work must have required a slow order. The BSL was dispatched out of Livingston throughout its history.

Considerable trouble has been experienced by our people in getting the conductors on train No. 3 to stop and let them off at Three Forks. M.J. Dignon was carried by to Sappington one night and Senator Tabor was threatened with the same treatment but decided not to be carried by, so Conductor Blank decided to let him off. We should advise the conductor in question (one seems to be making all the trouble) to look at his time card and in the future let passengers off without so many words or he will be applying for work on the section shortly.

Bozeman Chronicle **August 5, 1891**

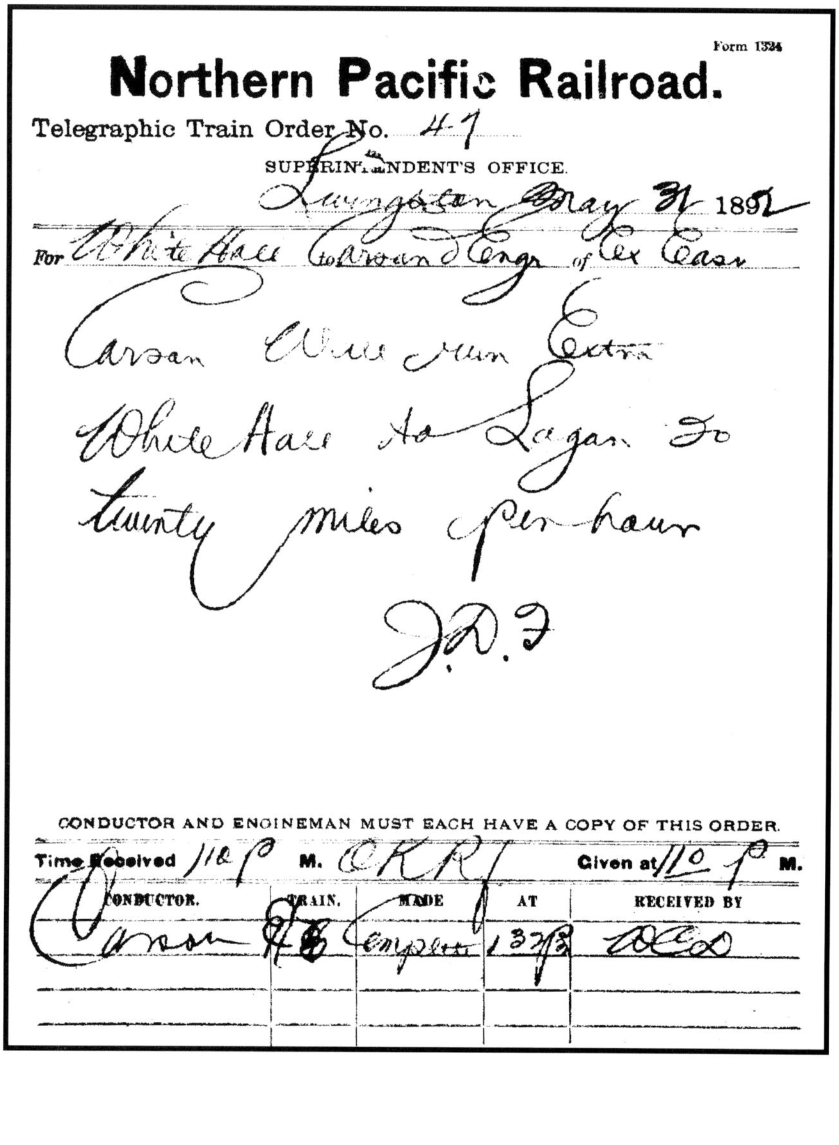

Northern Pacific Railroad. Form 1324

Telegraphic Train Order No. 4-1

SUPERINTENDENT'S OFFICE.

Livingston May 31 1892

For Whitehall Carson Engr of Ex Cars

Carson will run Extra
Whitehall to Logan 20
twenty miles per hour

J.D.J

CONDUCTOR AND ENGINEMAN MUST EACH HAVE A COPY OF THIS ORDER.

Time Received 110 P M. CKR Given at 110 P M.

CONDUCTOR.	TRAIN.	MADE	AT	RECEIVED BY
Carson	4 B	Empson	1 32/8	CCO

AP

Willow Creek:

Willow Creek at mile post 12 was a telegraph station, stock loading facility and loading site for agricultural products on the BSL. Located at the extreme western edge of the Gallatin Valley and along the Jefferson River, it is still in the heart of fertile farm land. It also served some large cattle ranches.

During his trip west, Captain Lewis named the tributaries of the Jefferson River for attributes he saw in the president. He named Willow Creek Philosophy River. The name was changed later to reflect the thick willows which grow along the banks.

When the territory was being surveyed to establish land ownership in the 1860's, the initial point (starting point) for the survey was set on a promontory overlooking

---

BRIDGE CARRIED AWAY

The passengers who came in on yesterday morning's train from Logan over the spur had a startling experience at Willow Creek, and some of them will feel "creepy" as long as they remember it. There is a short, but high bridge over the creek, which is about thirty [12] miles this side of Logan. A freshet resulting from the thaw on Tuesday had weakened the supports of the bridge by washing the earth away from the foundations. As the engine of No. 3 ran on this bridge the engineer felt the structure sway slightly and then begin to settle. The passengers felt it too, and they were thrown into a panic by the discovery, but almost before they could get out of their seats the train had passed over the bridge in safety. The engineer had pulled the throttle wide open and taken the bridge with a rush.

The train was brought to a standstill half a mile this side of the bridge and then backed up to the edge of the structure, which was floating away with the current.

Bozeman Chronicle   **April 15, 1891**

Willow Creek after being moved from the Beaverhead near Dillon.

While it was never a large community, the NP constructed a standard depot, stock yard and freight house; the local grain association built a grain elevator.

R.V. Nixon's father served as telegrapher here during the late 1920's. In February, 1909, a lamp in a Milwaukee dining car exploded at Willow Creek. Everyone evacuated the train, and the diner was completely destroyed.

This 1910 postcard view looks down the Jefferson River near a place later known as Ingleside Spur. The raw grade next to the river is the newly constructed Milwaukee, and the grade next to the cliff is that of the BSL. Willow Creek is in the distance. The NP did a realignment here, and the spur was the western end of the original curve. In the 1930's a wreck happened at Ingleside when an eastbound hit some soft grade.

On the Jefferson River, near Willow Creek, Mont.

Sappington:

This September, 1980, photo looks west from Sappington. The left track is the RB&P line to Harrison and the wye lead. The center track is the interchange track with the Milwaukee. The right track is the BSL main line to Butte. The Milwaukee diamond can be seen just beyond the switch. There once was a brick interlocking tower here. Bridge 19 is beyond the diamond. In the distance is the entrance to Jefferson Canyon.

Sappington at mile post 19 was named for H.H. Sappington, a local rancher. It served as the materials headquarters for the construction of the Red Bluff & Pony in 1889-90. Keefe & Green, the general contractors for the BSL, also built the RB&P. It was an NP&M project too.

Conditions were always primitive. J.W. Sutton, materials clerk at Sappington, wrote to E.H. McHenry, chief engineer on June 13, 1890,

The section House is now occupied by section crews, and in consequence, I have had to vacate the room I have used up to date. Will you kindly instruct me where I can obtain sleeping quarters, at your earliest convenience. I presume that as soon as the operating dept. occupies the depot I will have to move my desk & effects elsewhere.

On July 1st he again writes,

In regard to office & sleeping accommodations at Sappington. I would say, that with present arrangements, it is most difficult to do any work or obtain any sleep, as my desk is now, together with my bed, located in the main waiting room of depot, the small partition we

had, having been removed by Operating Dept. At Logan, I could obtain good accommodation, and could procure a room at rate of $4.50 per week, my board would amount to $5.50. I should be much obliged if you could make some arrangements for me at your earliest convenience & advise.

As primitive as it was, it was apparently better than Three Forks. M.J. Dignon complained on April 15, 1891, that the conductor on #3 bypassed Three Forks, which only had a box car as a depot, and left him off at Sappington. Senator Tabor was threatened with the same treatment.

In 1908 the Milwaukee built through and crossed the BSL at Sappington. A brick interlocking tower was built to protect the lines. Some traffic was interchanged between the two roads, and passenger trains were sometimes diverted to the other line when the home road's mountain tracks were closed.

Today a talc processing plant has been built at Sappington, and the Milwaukee is gone. The RB&P has been reduced to a branch ending at Harrison which sees intermittent service to a grain elevator. No railroad buildings remain.

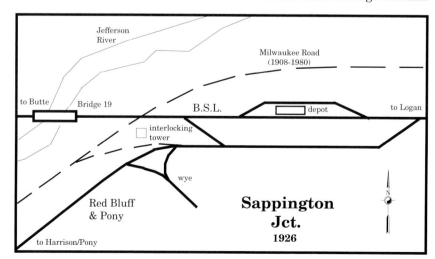

The Red Bluff & Pony:

MHS

The Red Bluff & Pony was built simultaneously with the BSL by the same contractors and funded by the same consortium. It connected the newly developing mining region around Pony with the smelters in Butte. The line was completed to Norris but never built beyond that point. At Harrison a branch was built to Pony. The Northern Pacific operating department took control of the line June 14, 1890, the same day it took over the BSL. J.C. Patterson was project engineer for both lines. This photo, taken by Hunter, looks down on Pony in May, 1904. It shows the end of the branch, the depot, and Haynes' photographic car, seen in many of his railroad photos. Today the extensions from Harrison to Pony and Norris have both been taken up, but Montana Rail Link still serves Harrison on a sporadic basis.

ON THE ROAD TO PONY

Progress of Railroad Building In That Part of Madison County

Red Bluff, March 18.- [Special correspondence of the Miner.]- In my Pony letter I forgot to say anything about the railroad. How this could happen after my experience in getting to that camp is hard to conceive. When I left Butte I expected to be set down in Harrison, six miles from Pony, on the following day. On arriving at Logan, the point where the Butte branch of the Northern Pacific leaves the main line, I was informed by the gentlemanly agent that no train would go to Harrison for three or four days. The track was in bad condition, he said, and would have to be repaired before trains could run over it.

Logan is not a very inviting loafing place. I venture to say that the most con-

firmed vagrant in Butte would be fired with something very nearly approaching ambition should he ever visit Logan.... And no vag has yet been born who would not desire to escape from the dreary solitude of Logan, or who would lack the determination to set his legs in motion to accomplish that end. The only habitation in the place are the depot, the waiting room of which is guiltless of a seat of any kind, and a miserable shack which charity would blush to call a hotel. I ate one meal there, and believe the next one would have starved me to death.

Taking the transfer wagon I was driven six miles across the country and was landed in Three Forks, when a lay over till next morning was compulsory. Comfortable quarters were found at the Three Forks hotel ... time did not hang heavily on my hands.

The Anaconda company have purchased 5,000 acres of land here, and if the monster refining and reduction works they contemplate building are located at this place,

a great change will be wrought in two years.... [*The smelter was built at Great Falls instead.*]

Leaving Three Forks in the morning, I rode twenty-eight miles in a spring wagon over a rough road, and landed in Pony at 4 o'clock in the evening. There I met a party of engineers and gleaned the following facts in regard to the branch railroad. The line from Sappington, on the Jefferson to Red Bluff, a distance of about twenty miles, is graded to within three miles of the bluff, with the exception of a long trestle work across Norwegian gulch, which will require several weeks to complete. The track is laid a short distance beyond Harrison, but the road was not ballasted and was impassable at the time.

At Harrison, seven miles from Pony, a branch puts off for the latter place, and the grade was completed last fall with the exception of a swamp crossing, where piles will have to be driven. The contractors are on the ground....

Butte Daily Miner   **March 18, 1890**

Jefferson Bar (Cavern-Danmor & Hubbard):

.JVM

In 1881 the Utah & Northern surveyed through Jefferson Canyon for a proposed line to Helena. Five miles of grade were constructed as part of that effort. After the 1882 agreement for the U&N to meet the NP at Garrison, the Jefferson route was left neglected. When the NP proposed the BSL, the UP reopened the work on this route. After some violence and negotiations, the NP ended up with the UP grade through Jefferson Canyon and the 15 miles of completed line. Consequently, construction through the canyon went very quickly.

At mile post 26 there were extensive placer diggings across the river. The NP put in the siding of Jefferson Bar. Some difficulties were encountered when the washings from the hydraulic mining caused the river to threaten the railroad grade.

The siding was renamed Danmor after 1909 to recognize Dan Morrison who discovered Lewis & Clark Caverns on the hillside above. While hunting, he had noticed a flight of birds which seemed to rise up out of the ground. Intrigued, he investigated and found the entrance to the cave. Originally known as Morrison's Cave, it was discovered that William Clark of the famous expedition had climbed the same mountain to view the river during the journey to the coast, and the caverns were later named in the expedition's honor.

Morrison developed the cave as a tourist attraction, and a siding named Hubbard was put in at mile post 25, the Morrison Ranch, for tourist trains. This siding was taken up by 1926.

The cave turned out to be on railroad land, and in 1911 the Northern Pacific donated the cave and the land surrounding it to the federal government. It is now known as the Lewis & Clark Caverns National Monument.

A west bound NCL rounds the corner west of Jefferson Bar (Danmor) in the late 1920's. The siding can be seen in the foreground. Lewis & Clark Caverns are just behind the photographer. Across the river were the London Hills and placer diggings.

NORTHERN PACIFIC DONATES HISTORIC CAVERN TO PUBLIC

The Northern Pacific railway has conveyed to the United States government 160 acres of land adjoining its right of way in Jefferson county to enable the government to perpetuate the Lewis and Clark Cavern National monument....

The cavern is at a point about one mile northwest of Lime Spur station, on the Northern Pacific main line, between Logan and Butte. In a letter under date of March 2, 1911, the secretary of the interior expresses deep appreciation of the action of the Northern Pacific railway "in thus enabling the government to preserve for the free enjoyment of all the people the great cavern within this tract."

It is not yet known what steps the government will take to make the interior of the cavern accessible to the public, but it is expected that it will be equipped with a stairway as far as it is practicable for visitors to descend, and the various formations suitably protected.

Missoulian   **April 23, 1911**

Lime Spur:

The following article was published in the Spring, 1997, Society for Industrial Archaeology Klepetko Chapter Newsletter. It is a condensation of an article published in the February, 1930, Mining and Metallurgy.

At Lime Spur, Mont. the East Butte Copper Mining Co. has been quarrying limestone for twenty years. The quarry is beside the Northern Pacific R.R. in the Jefferson River canyon, 4 1/2 miles east of Cardwell, Montana.

History:
This quarry was opened in 1900 by Dan Morrison of Whitehall, the discoverer of the Morrison cave, to supply a demand for smelter flux. Limestone was sold to the Pittsmont smelter of the East Butte Copper Mining Co. and to the Butte Reduction Works. As no particular effort was made at the quarry to select the rock, that delivered to the smelters was unduly high in magnesia and impurities. The East Butte Co., therefore, bought the quarry in 1909 and confined operations to the high-grade beds in order to supply rock of the desired purity for its own smelter and the Butte Reduction Works. It also developed a market for some of its rock with the beet sugar factories. The latter market increased until in later years all rock, larger than 4 inches was being shipped to the sugar factories, and smaller than 4 inches was being used as flux in the blast furnaces at the Pittsmont smelter. In 1924, the East Butte concluded a contract with the Anaconda company for the treatment of its ores, and the Pittsmont smelter was shut down, which made the minus 4 inch rock a useless by-product. Since there was not enough revenue in the sugar rock alone and because of limited waste room, it became necessary to increase the proportion of plus 4 inch rock and to develop a market for the minus 4 inch.

The plus 4 inch rock was increased by the elimination of all crushing until after the separation of sugar rock, any necessary breaking of large boulders being done by men with 16-lb. hammers, by bulldozing, and by using more care in the primary blasting, being careful to take advantage of seams and cracks. Originally the small rock constituted 60-65% of the production; today it amounts to 44%. Fifty percent of the reduction, however, can be attributed to a reduction in minimum size to 3 inches allowed by the sugar factory.

In order to develop a market for the minus 4 inch, a crushing and screening plant to size this rock for concrete aggregate and road construction was added to the original plant. This rock is now being used extensively in most of the construction and road building around Butte.

The quarry has produced, since the East Butte acquired ownership, 1,200,000 tons of rock. At times, on account of its purity, limestone is sold to a glass factory at Lovell, Wyo. The concrete aggregate is acceptable to, and passes all Federal aid specifications for highway and bridge construction.

Geology:
At Lime Spur and vicinity, in the Jefferson Range, there is a fault block about 3 by 4 miles in area, exposing the Madison and overlying Quadrant and Ellis formations, which have been folded by pressure from the north into a great arch with axis trending southwest by west. It is bounded on the north by an overthrust fault, on the north side of which is the Belt formation, and on the east and south sides by another overthrust fault, on the east and south side of which , respectively, the Three Forks formation, of Devonian age and the Livingston formation of Cretaceous age. The Jefferson river here flows east and west and has cut a deep canyon in the north limb of the arch through the Ellis and Quadrant formations and into the Madison, the beds of which strike north 70 degrees to 45 degrees east, thus forming the prominent cliffs of Madison limestone on both sides of the river. The Madison formation consists of 325 feet of laminated limestone at the base, then 350 feet of massively bedded limestone, then 575 feet of jaspery cherty limestone at the top. The Lime Spur quarry is in one of the upper beds of the massively bedded portion... [a number] of quarries are in the same formation.

A LAND SLIDE

The Butte and Bozeman branch of the Northern Pacific was on Thursday night the scene of an accident, which might have been frightful in its result. The train while going at a good rate of speed ran into a land slide near Lime Spur. It was the Pony express and struck the slide at about half past twelve o'clock, about a mile and a half west of Lime Spur. The line at this point runs along the edge of the mountains, and to make the situation double dangerous the slide occurred on a curve, thirty feet above the river. Fortunately when the engine left the track it turned toward the mountain, thus avoiding disaster to the whole train which would have been precipitated into the river. The engine, several cars and all the passengers were badly shaken up; but no one seriously injured. The conductor went to Sappington and warned No. 3 which was late and it is lucky it was; it would have reached the slide first.

Bozeman Chronicle   **August 5, 1891**

Jefferson Island (Cardwell):

Operator Clifford Brown stands in front of the Cardwell depot in this 1928 photograph. He formerly worked at Whitehall and Homestake.

As Sappington is the eastern entrance to Jefferson Canyon, Cardwell at mile post 31 is the western entrance. It was originally named Jefferson Island. When the Milwaukee Road built along the river in 1908, it was renamed Cardwell to avoid confusion. The Milwaukee had also named their station, just across the river, Jefferson Island.

While never amounting to much, Cardwell had at one time figured largely in NP plans to build a line up the Boulder River to connect with the HBV&B and then into Butte via Calvin. Until Kendrick became chief engineer in 1888, the plan was to build through the canyon on the present alignment, then turn northwest at Jefferson Island (Cardwell). The line would have actually connected with the HBV&B's Elkhorn branch at Finn siding. General Anderson's departure shelved those plans, however, and despite many published accounts promising its imminent construction, the Boulder River line was never built. Kendrick, who had a reputation as being in favor of "short lines," elected to build the new Gallatin-Butte line via the shortest route available--directly west from Whitehall and over the continental divide at Homestake Pass following an original 1871 survey.

Engine #583, J. Frost engineer, broke a crosshead at Jefferson Island Sunday morning; the train crew came up to Whitehall on a handcar, and Engineer McGonigle was called out to bring in the train--No. 59.

Engine #583 was disconnected on one side, and ran back light to Bozeman. There is too much Frost around the engine this cold weather, and is liable to break most anything. Jack Frost is a Jonah to the ranchman as well as to the railroad. Savey, Jack? [*Obviously, there is more to this story*].

Jefferson Valley Zephyr

January 11, 1895

Whitehall:

JVM

This photo of Whitehall, taken from the coal tower, can be dated to before 1895. The two stall engine house at the center right burned in that year and was replaced by a four stall roundhouse farther to the south. The 1890 depot stands in the distance and was still in place in 1997. One can see the water tower, stock yards and newly developing businesses along "Railroad Avenue."

Whitehall at mile post 38 is the largest town on the Butte Short Line except for Butte. Its history is that of the railroad. On September 26, 1889, the Northern Pacific paid $777 to the Brooke family for 45 acres to construct a yard and roundhouse for the maintenance and repair of helper engines working the hill.

The Brooke family requested that the station be named Whitehall after the stage station Mr. Brooke operated up Whitetail Creek north of the railroad. Mr. Brooke's son-in-law Robert Noble had a town site surveyed and the plat was officially recorded August 23, 1890. The Northern Pacific also developed and later sold lots in a Whitehall subdivision.

This postcard view of Whiteall is from between 1905 and 1910. Many changes have taken place in the past 10-15 years. The most noticeable are the grain elevator, the stock yard and the store fronts.

WRM

The four stall Whitehall roundhouse is shown in this 1911 photograph. It was built in 1895 after the two stall engine house burned down. Locomotive 31 is a Y class 2-8-0 built by Alco in 1898. #131 is a S-2 class 4-6-0 built in 1900.   The 3100 is a Z-1 class 2-6-6-2 built in 1910 and later sold to the Polson Logging Co. Pictured also are some of the crewmen. Left to right: "Pus" Hanscomb, Mike Wentz, unknown, C. Mikesell, Bill Hamm, Harry Young and Bill Mosier.

Fires plagued Whitehall in the early years. The first two stall roundhouse burned down in 1895 and was replaced with a four stall one. In 1912 a fire virtually destroyed all of the main street buildings. In 1916 another fire destroyed the original runway to the top of the coal tower, leading to the replacement of the whole structure.

One hundred and ten men appeared on the Northern Pacific's Whitehall employment roles in 1900. The payroll amounted to $6,000 a month, and in the 1890's the wages were paid in cash brought to town by a payroll car. The arrival of the paymaster was an occasion for celebration.

Railroad jobs at the turn of the century were dangerous. In August, 1891, engineer J.T. Getchel on locomotive #161 leaned out of his cab window to check the running gear as he passed over a switch. The switch stand staff struck his head and pulled him from the cab. He fell to the ties with a dislocated shoulder and numerous cuts and bruises. He had to be taken to the hospital in Bozeman because Whitehall as yet had no doctor.

In November, 1891, a brakeman was riding a coal car to the top of the tower when a coupling broke pushing his car over the edge. He jumped for it as the car crashed to the ground breaking in two. Luckily he was uninjured.

Later, a caboose broke loose at Homestake and ran down the mountain. A message was sent ahead to Whitehall, and the switch was thrown for the Gaylord. The caboose stopped near Parrot.

Foreman C.C. Parker looks pretty rocky since the roundhouse burned. We think C.C. does not fancy standing out in nature's roundhouse wiping off the "hog." C.C. says he does not like to have the Montana zephyrs blow through his sideburns.

Jefferson Valley Zephyr January 11, 1895

JVM

The perch of several Whitehall photographers, both the old coal tower and the new one under construction are shown in the phtotograph at right.

An early train makes a stop at Whitehall in this undated photograph. #721 is a 4-4-0 American type loco.

One of the worst wrecks on the BSL happened just west of Whitehall on July 10, 1923. Two boys were returning from a swim in Pipestone Creek. They were walking along the tracks near Blackstone Spur (mile post 42) when one 11 year-old decided to show the other how easy it was to break the lock with a rock and throw the switch. He had no more than begun when they looked up in horror to see west bound passenger train #41 approaching at speed. It was running late He tried to throw the switch back, but it was too late. The train was side-tracked into the 200' long spur. Before the locomotive and 12 passenger cars could be stopped, they hit the end of the spur and crashed. The locomotive's crew, Albert Jacobs, W.J. Bouillard and Clifford Marney, were immediately killed. Engineer Tom Barry was pinned by his leg between the stoker plate and the elevator in the engine.

Witnesses summoned help immediately. Dr. Packard wanted to amputate Barry's leg in order to be able to remove him, but Barry refused. In a matter of time he bled to death in the cab despite efforts to extricate him with acetylene torches.

People did not often remain long in Whitehall due to being bumped by others through union seniority systems. For example, Ron Nixon's father served as agent in Whitehall from 1921 through 1924 and then moved to Willow Creek.

Whitehall became more of a railroad town when the line to the Parrot smelter was built in 1896 and was extended all the way to Alder in 1902. When the Milwaukee built through in 1908, their tracks passed two miles south at Piedmont where a substation was built as a part of electrification in 1914. Piedmont served as the eastern terminus for the Butte helpers assisting Milwaukee trains over Pipestone pass.

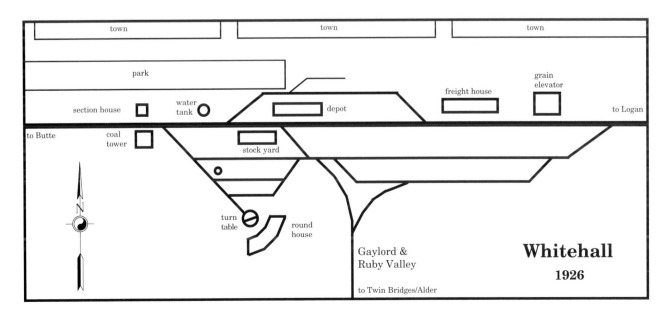

Winter in Whitehall

This early view of the round house in Whitehall in winter, taken from the engine lead, shows how cold it can get in this high mountain valley. Notice the ice hanging from the water tower. The boiler in the round house is working hard to keep the heat up. The town is to the left of the photo.

JVM

Locomotive #598 sits in Whitehall after a push up the mountain during the winter of 1910. While heavy snow is unusual on the east side of Homestake, snow plows were used occasionally.

As of 1997 the 1890 depot still stood in Whitehall. Painted in BN white and green, boarded up and in sad repair, the graceful eaves and decorative bracing reminds one of days gone by. The building is owned by MRL, but it is in the process of being sold. Various plans have been put forward for it.

The Gaylord & Ruby Valley:

Several companies surveyed routes to connect the Beaverhead and Jefferson Valleys through Dillon and Twin Bridges. The first was the Utah & Northern in 1881. Some grade south of Whitehall was constructed before the route was abandoned.

In 1893 Samuel Word, who had been important in the development of the RF&CC, announced the incorporation of the Helena & Southern Railroad. Twenty miles of grade were finished before the project was discontinued in May of 1894. The Montana & Southeastern Railroad also looked at a line connecting Dillon to Butte over Pipestone Pass, and the Elliston and Southern proposed a line down the Boulder River. None of these lines was built.

The Northern Pacific surveyed south from Whitehall in 1892. In 1896 a smelter was built south of Whitehall at Point of Rock later called Parrot. The NP built a line to the smelter, and the town of Gaylord grew where the railroad crossed the Jefferson River. Population warranted additional construction in the upper valley, and, in 1897, the Gaylord & Ruby Valley was chartered. The NP acquired the former grades of the previously failed projects, and the NP crews laid a mile of track a day southward. The first train made its way into Twin Bridges August 1, 1897.

The railroad planned to build to Virginia City, the center of a rich mining district, and by May 5, 1902, the construction reached Alder on the Ruby River. Unfortunately, this was as far as the road would ever go. While various plans to complete the road to Virginia City and to build a branch to Dillon were put forward, none was funded by the railroad.

Operations on the G&RV were sporadic and seasonal. By 1910 service was curtailed to three trains a week.

One interesting story involves a south bound train in 1920. Engineer Barry noticed that a car behind the locomotive had caught fire. Thinking fast, he uncoupled the car from the rest of the train leaving the passenger coach and several irate passengers behind. The locomotive and car sped into Twin Bridges, and the crew began dousing the car with water. Soon a crowd gathered to watch the activity. Suddenly, conductor Howard remembered there was dynamite on the car. The crowd was dispersed. When the locomotive and crew returned for the stranded coach, passengers were mollified when they learned there had been dynamite on the car. Luckily no one was injured on the train or in Twin Bridges.

Pipestone Springs (Pipestone):

JVM

Pipestone Springs Hotel, Pipestone Springs, Mont.   2027

Pipestone Hot Springs Hotel is shown about 1907. Built out of brick in 1906, it replaced an earlier structure. A fire, caused by a lady leaving a burning candle in the dressing room of the baths, destroyed this structure in 1913. Its replacement burned again in 1918. Only a few out buildings remain today.

Seven miles west of Whitehall at mile post 45 is the siding of Pipestone. It is the first siding on the ascending grade of the eastern approach to Homestake Pass.

Located about a mile south of the railroad siding are some natural hot springs along the banks of Big Pipestone Creek. In the 1890's the springs were developed as a resort primarily for the people of Butte and Anaconda who wanted to escape the smokey confines of the cities. Excursion trains brought visitors from both as often as twice a day during the season although other trains would also stop to leave people off for the spa. A horse-drawn wagon with seats built along the sides and a top to keep off the rain would meet guests at the primitive depot and transport them to the resort.

In 1906 a modern structure was built to accommodate the growing business. Guest cabins, tents, a plunge, a mud bath and an indoor bathhouse were also built. The owners sold bottled water with "healing properties."

One interesting tale about the resort involves a Mrs. Fan Packard, a school teacher in Whitehall in 1911. Mrs. Pack-

ard and three other teachers, who were used to finer things back east, would hop the Saturday morning train to Pipestone to "have a bath, rub down, our fingernails fixed up, a shampoo and set." They would then return to Whitehall on the noon train in time for lunch.

An Anaconda Co. attorney named Roy S. Alley bought the complex in 1912. Within a year the main hotel burned. He replaced it with another which also contained a post office and a dance hall. In 1918 this structure burned. The last replacement was more modest with only nine guest rooms. An outdoor dance pavilion

was added, however. A fossil bed located near the hotel was visited by agents from the Smithsonian.

In later years a golf course was added, but modern transportation and the decay of the facilities began to take their toll. Most of the structures were razed. For a time the outdoor pool remained open, but in the 1950's the resort closed.

The first depot at Pipestone siding was a boxcar, but by 1908 the NP had built a small depot and an ice house as well. A section was located north of the siding. Today nothing remains. MRL has opened a ballast pit a mile above Pipestone which has become the western end of their operations.

SOME SUNDAY SIFTINGS

A Car Jumps a Track on a Trestle on the Homestake Route

Pipestone Springs as a Sunday Resort - Its Lake and Its Baths - Bottling Mineral Water.

Saturday night a train broke in two on a high trestle near Beefstraight on the Northern Pacific between this city and Pipestone. In crossing the trestle the air was applied to the brakes. In the center of the train was a light car which bounded when the air was applied and got off the track. It was not a very pleasant position for the train hands, who expected that a good portion of the train might yet fall over the bank. The front half of the train was taken to Butte .... It was a bad place to have such an accident happen, and none realize this more than the train hands.

The brakeman on the stub train which runs between here and Logan, while walking along the trestle near the scene of Saturday night's little wreck mis-stepped and fell through. It was only the narrowness of the space between the ties that saved him from certain death. He was caught in the stomach and though slightly shaken up was not otherwise injured.

The NP has made an excursion rate for the benefit of Butte people of $1 for the round trip between here and Pipestone Springs. The only thing now left for the company to do would be to put on a Sunday train that would accommodate excursion parties.... Should this Sunday train be put on Pipestone would very deservedly soon become one of the most popular of the many Sunday resorts within an hour's reach of Butte.

A large number of people are now recuperating at Pipestone and it is evident that the accommodations will soon have to be increased.....

An industry that gives promise of great success is being inaugurated at Pipestone and by the Fourth of July, Pipestone mineral water will take the place of Idaho water over the refreshment bars. "Bob" Thomas now has the machinery necessary for charging and bottling the water, and men competent to know pronounce it better than the water shipped here from Idaho or Minnesota. Being a home industry the enterprise is receiving much encouragement and Mr. Thomas has already been guaranteed the patronage of several big Butte business houses, who would like to see this take the place of the imported mineral water, in the interest of home industry. Mr. Thomas says he can put the water up as cheaply as anybody can, and will have the advantage of cheap freight rates....

Inter Mountain   **June 24, 1891**

This early view overlooks the lake and the resort complex. Canoes and rowboats are on the lake. The railroad skirts the hills in the distance. A wagon met the trains and brought guests to the resort. JVM

Guests relax outside of their tent cottages near Pipestone Springs in this postcard view dated 1908. Wooden cabins later replaced the tents.

This interior bathhouse view postcard was mailed from the Pipestone post office in 1910. This and the main hotel burned in 1913 but were rebuilt shorty afterward.

Spire Rock:

Spire Rock siding looks rather forlorn in this 1995 photo. The building pushed over at left is the telephone booth. The side track is at left in this north looking view. Spire Rock itself stands in the distance. Omsun's Spur is just around the ridge in the distance as is bridge 51 where the water tank was located in earlier days. A telegraph office was built here in 1909, and three boxcars were used as habitation by the operators. The office was removed in 1947. The 1929 ICC valuation report lists a stock chute here, but it is not clear if it was here at the siding or at Omsun's Spur.

Spire Rock siding is located at mile post 50 just after one enters the big loop going upgrade. Originally Spire Rock was located 1.4 miles to the west at Bridge 51. In 1890 a water tank was built there fed by a ditch from Halfway Creek. The section house was also located there as well as several dwellings for families.

As part of the upgrade done at the turn of the century, a 2,905 foot siding was built to the east where there was more room. After that Spire Rock had a rather split identity. The section and tank continued to be at the old location, but the telegraph office was at the new. The operator at Spire Rock could actually see the Welch telegraph office just across the loop and several hundred feet above him. Between the two they controlled all movement in the Little Pipestone Creek Valley.

Between the two was Omsun's Spur (mile post 51). Records are

unclear, but Omsun's Spur was very short and apparently used only for stock loading. Little evidence of it remains.

Overlooking all of the railroad sites on the east side of Homestake is Spire Rock itself. The massive granite upthrust dominates the scenery in the big loop and for miles around. Two smaller cousins, one of which is Pipestone Rock, can be seen in many photos. Wherever one is in the big loop, Spire Rock serves as a gigantic landmark as can be seen in photos of the day.

ECHOES OF THE RAIL

Conerning "Throttle-Pullers", Firemen, Ticket-Punchers, "Brakies," etc

Jimmie and Nellie Deeney [son and daughter of Spire Rock section foreman Barney Deeney] of the Spire Rock section house, started down the hill on a handcar Saturday night. When in the vicinity of Pipestone Springs, and while coming at a speed rate of about 20 miles an hour, a cow was met coming head on, with no lights or signals, and unfortunately Jimmie had left his cow catcher at home when they pulled out from the Rock. Jimmie tooted his whistle and applied the air -- he had lots of air for both he and his sister were strictly in it speedily -- but without avail, and the first thing he and Miss Deeney knew they were pulling themselves together at the bottom of a 20-foot rock-filled embankment, one on each side. Fortunately, both escaped with nothing more serious than sprains and bruises. Jimmie constituted himself a wrecking crew, got the car on the track again and completed their journey without further mishaps. The cow's side of the story has not yet been heard.

Jefferson Valley Zephyr   **January 18, 1895**

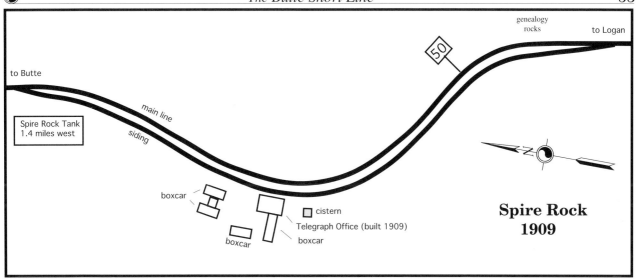

to Butte

main line

siding

Spire Rock Tank
1.4 miles west

boxcar

boxcar

boxcar

cistern

Telegraph Office (built 1909)

genealogy rocks

to Logan

50

**Spire Rock
1909**

Spire Rock Genealogy

People writing their names on rocks around Butte has apparently always been a tradition. At many places on Homestake Pass one can find where NP railroad personnel wrote theirs also.

Imagine waiting in the hole at Spire Rock for a westbound that is late in arriving. Nothing to do but cool your heels while you wait. Well, there is one thing you can do. You can take a track spike and

a maul from the engine and carve your name on the granite boulders all around you.

Here and at various other places on the mountain one can find where generations of NP trainmen have recorded their presence on the BSL.

It was not easy either. The authors tried it and gave up before they managed to get even their last name carved. The granite is a lot harder than it looks.

But keep your eyes peeled if you are walking the mountain. The rocks have a story to tell about the people who served the railroad in this very remote place.

The photo above shows a rock at the east switch of Spire Rock siding. L. Goble's name appears prominantly. Mr. Goble began service on the NP in 1949 and made the transition to BN in 1970.

The rock at right has an older story to tell. According to NP seniority records, T.E. Bequette for example, began his service with the NP in 1909, carved his name here in 1914, and retired from the NP in 1958 after 49 years of service.

Omson's Spur:

Omsun's Spur was located at milepost 51. Almost nothing remains at this location. The spur is listed in the 1893 timetable as capable of holding 15 cars. What purpose it served is unclear, but it existed until the 1920's. Perhaps it served as a stock loading spur. A tie gang worked here during construction. Mile post 51 now marks the western limit of Montana Rail Link's ownership. This photo looks back at the west switch of Spire Rock from near where Omsun's Spur was located.

Spire Rock Tank:

This early postcard view shows Spire Rock Tank and Viaduct. The bridge was rebuilt out of steel in 1901. The tank and section house stood at the east end of the bridge. Several families lived here at one time. A 7,600' ditch brought water to the tank from up Half way Creek. Shortly after this photo was taken Spire Rock siding was built one mile to the east. Omsun's Spur is around the corner to the right.

Bridge 51 (Spire Rock Viaduct):

Above is the authors' attempt to duplicate the postcard view at left. The tank is gone and the trees are taller, but the bridge looks just the same in 1996 as it did right after the turn of the century. Spire Rock Viaduct crosses Halfway Creek.

Bridge 51 is one of two large steel bridges on the east side of Homestake Pass. Located within a mile of each other, they span Halfway Creek and Big Pipestone Creek respectively at the head end of the big loop.

Bridge 51, Spire Rock Viaduct, takes its name from the rocky outcrop that dominates the skyline above it. In 1889 it was constructed of wood. Built by Matthews & Co. of St. Paul, it was one of those that held up the completion of the BSL.

In 1901, as part of a general upgrade of the line, it was replaced by the straight steel structure seen above. It is 580' long with ten 40 foot spans and three 60 foot spans and is the second longest of the three steel bridges remaining on the mountain. It is of double plate girder construction, is unballasted and has no pedestrian walkway.

Unlike Bridge 52, it can be seen from various places in the loop as well as from the Delmo Lake Road, the primary road access to the area.

Originally the Spire Rock section house was located at the eastern approach, and a small community of several families inhabited cabins in the gulch beyond. The tank apparently lasted into

The builder's plate on Bridge 51.

the 1920's as it is still listed on the 1929 ICC property valuation survey. The water stop moved from here to Welch, however, after the construction of the cistern and water column at Beef Straight Creek (Welch). The bridge remained in very good condition in 1997 although some bridge timbers had been stolen and ramps had been built by ATV riders.

Bridge 52 (Big Pipestone Creek Viaduct):

A Steel Trussel on the Northern Pacific Railway.

The postcard view at right shows Bridge 52 over Big Pipestone Creek. The west end of the bridge is the actual head of the big loop. The loop bends back so tightly on itself here that the engine crews and caboose crews on long trains could wave at each other. The rocky outcrop behind the bridge is unnamed on Forest Service maps.

Bridge 52 is Big Pipestone Viaduct on the railroad profiles. It is a 500' long double plate girder bridge similar in construction to its two partners on the mountain. It is a straight access bridge except for the final 100' which begins a tight curve to the south toward Welch and the upper leg of the big loop. It has eight 40 foot spans and three 60 foot spans. It is the shortest of the three steel bridges.

This is the most inaccessible of the three. It cannot be seen from very far away at all, and the only road is a jeep trail ending on top of a ridge above the bridge. Few photographs exist of trains on this bridge until much later when W.R. McGee captured a stock train with helpers on Bridge 52 from his vantage point on the roof walks.

Like Bridge 51, it was originally constructed of wood and replaced by this steel bridge in 1902. There do not appear to have been any settlements near here except for a Parrot Quarry Spur which appears on a map attached to a 1899 mining claim. Evidence on the ground indicates it was a short spur to load granite half a mile to the east of the bridge. Railroad records studied by the authors do not show it.

This is the country into which the would-be robbers disappeared after their abortive holdup attempt at Welch in 1907 during which engineer Clow was shot and killed and fireman Sullivan was wounded. One can clearly see why the search dogs lost their trail.

The general condition of the bridges, ties and rails remains good around both Bridges 51 and 52. A rain storm in 1994 washed the fills badly, and many loads of dirt would have to be brought in to make the line pass inspection. In the late 1970's BN marked many rocks through here with white paint indicating they would have to be cut away to allow for the passage of modern trains of 80-90 foot long cars.

This 1996 photo shows the west end of Bridge 52 which is the actual head of the big loop. The curve at the west end of the bridge begins the upper leg. As one can see in the postcard photo above, the loop here is very tight. The terrain between bridges 51 & 52 is rugged featuring deep cuts and tight corners. There does not appear to have been any settlements at this location other than a quarry referred to in mining records as Parrot Quarry Spur. It does not seem to be on NP time tables of the day. The view from the middle of this bridge is magnificent.

Beef Straight:

Peak and Curve at Summit of the Rockies, on the N. P. R. R. near Butte, Mont.

The first siding on the upper leg of the loop in 1890 was Beef Straight siding at mile post 53.7. It took its name from the creek half a mile to the west. The special instructions to the 1893 timetable say, "When Nos. 3 and 4 meet at 'Beef Straight.' No. 4 will take siding." It lists the siding capacity as 15 cars.

In 1899 a 1.1 mile long spur was built to Welch Quarry a mile to the west. A year later a 65 car siding was built from the quarry switch west and named Welch after the developer of the quarry. By 1902 Beef Straight was reduced to a single-ended spur with a capacity of 12 cars, and it was removed a short time later.

It was below Pipestone Rock in the middle of Bridge 54 that the final spike ceremony took place on March 29, 1890. The name Pipestone is attributed to Native Americans who made tobacco pipes out of the local clay. Many people viewing Pipestone Rock from this angle mistake it for Spire Rock.

This early postcard view shows the location of Beef Straight siding (above the grade on the hill) after it was taken out about 1905. The back side of Pipestone Rock can be seen in the distance. Beef Straight Creek and Welch are just to the left. Welch's Quarry is on the other side of Pipestone Rock. Despite the postcard's caption, Beef Straight is six miles from the summit at Homestake.

Spire Rock at Summit of the Rockies, near Butte, Mont., on the N. P. R. R.

The view at left shows the scenery at mile post 54 below Welch. The sign can be seen in the photo. The view is from north of Beef Straight. Spire Rock is in the distance across the big loop. Bridges 51 & 52 are between here and the rocky outcrop. Tight corners, big bridges, boulders, 2.2% grades and beautiful scenery are the features along this part of the Butte Short Line.

Welch:

This faded photo taken from a moving train bears the caption "Welch, Mont." It was taken sometime after 1903 and shows the telegraph station, box car living quarters, order board and tool shed. These buildings and all but the last 200 feet of the west end of the side track are gone today.

Welch siding, located at mile post 54.7, is five miles below the summit on the east side of the pass. It is at about the midway point on the upper leg of the big loop, and Spire Rock siding, Spire Rock, Bridge 51, Whitehall and the Tobacco Root Mountains can be seen to the north and east across the valley. From Welch one could see west bound trains beginning the 2.2% grade at Pipestone siding ten rail miles away and watch their progress for much of their journey.

Welch siding was built in 1900 and replaced Beef Staight a mile to the east. Welch was named for James Welch who developed a granite quarry at the end of a spur a mile up Beef Straight Creek from the station. The siding was needed to spot cars brought down from the quarry.

In 1901 a telegraph station was built which served as the order station on the east side for many years. The 1910 census indicates Harry B. Day and his wife Edith served as telegraphers/operators. They had two children. It similarly lists Joseph E. Reed as a telegrapher/operator who boarded with Days. This arrangement would cover the three shifts. The census indicates about 20 people worked in the quarry including a locomotive engineer and fireman.

In 1906 a post office was opened. James Welch served as its first postmaster.

The 1919 Interstate Commerce Commission property valuation for section 13 lists the following structures at Welch: a 16' x 20' telegraph office without platform (see the photo above), two dwellings made from carbodies, a carbody ice house, and the water column on the other side of the creek (below bridge 54). Several foundations for quarry workers' cabins can still be seen above the spur switch.

The postcard at right, mailed in 1903, shows what was Bridge 54 and the water column. Compare this photo with the Haynes photo on page 22 taken only ten years earlier in 1893. The bridge has been recently filled in as part of the the upgrade. The water column has been constructed using a cistern fed by a flume from Beef Straight Creek. Pipestone Rock is in the background.

VIEW FROM WELCH, MONT. NEAR WHITEHALL, MONT.

The view at left was taken from the Welch depot platform looking north toward Pipestone Rock in 1910. The switch to the spur is behind the shed. Beef Straight Cr. and Bridge 54 are below Pipestone Rock. Welch's Quarry is up the drainage to the left.

The 1907 Holdup Near Welch:

Despite its remote location, interesting things happened at Welch. Without a doubt, the most exciting thing was the May 7, 1907, attempted holdup of the east bound North Coast Limited one mile west of the station. The story begins in Butte.

As a Burlington engine was added to #2 at Butte Transfer, George Towers and at least one other man climbed up between the tender and the express car with a satchel full of Giant powder. Frank Clow was the enginer and Tom Sullivan was the fireman that night. Clow was a veteran engineer and had some experience with attempted robberies. Four years before his train had been stopped at Skones by armed men who robbed the express car (see page 84).

At the scheduled time Clow and Sullivan started their train up the west side of the pass and crested the continental divide at Homestake about 1:00 AM . The two would-be robbers remained in hiding.

Near mile post 56 the stowaways crawled over the tender, and with drawn pistols they ordered Clow and Sullivan to stop the train. Their apparent intention was to blow up the express car's safe.

Clow appeared to comply, but he "dynamited" the brakes instead. This startled the two bandits. Both fired several shots from their revolvers, killing Clow and wounding Sullivan.

The rapid stopping of the train alarmed the rest of the train crew. Conductor Bert Culver and Sheriff Webb of Yellowstone County, who happened to be on board, ran toward the engine in the darkness. Their approach frightened the stick up men who jumped off the engine, fled into the rocks and ran down a gully below the tracks. Webb and a crewman followed in hot pursuit.

Meanwhile, a telegraph message was sent to Butte, and Sheriff Henderson left to take up the chase with a posse on a special train at about 5:00 AM. By the time the posse arrived at Welch, Webb had lost the trail after following the outlaws for over a mile in the darkness. He speculated the robbers had horses hidden nearby.

Webb arrested a man who had been found in the cab. He maintained he was just a tramp who had been riding the rods and had not been a part of the holdup attempt. He and Sullivan were able to give a description of the two men who had killed Clow.

NP officials sent another special train from Deer Lodge with prison trackers and bloodhounds. More Butte police loaded on it as it came through town, and they arrived at Welch about noon.

The country was very rough, however, and the dogs lost the trail. Officers telegraphed that they believed the two men were headed back toward Butte. The Northern Pacific immediately offered $2,000 reward for their capture.

Several days later, George Towers, Harry Gruber and George Hastings were arrested in Basin, Montana, for the crime. They subsequently were brought to trial. Towers claimed two other men did it, and he was innocent. Witnesses testified he matched the description of the taller of the two bandits, however, and despite the testimony of a lady from Butte who said he was with her all night, he was found guilty of murder.

Clow was heralded as a hero by the local press. It was discovered that his body had been riddled by five shots. Sullivan was wounded in the arm and survived by playing dead on the cab floor until the robbers fled. Clow's setting of the train brakes before his death, however, prevented the train from running away, and it was said he saved many lives in a selfless act of bravery. In his honor the NP later renamed a siding on the Helena line for him.

The Wreck of the NCL at Welch in 1922:

JVM

On March 17, 1922, this head on collision occured at Welch siding. Train #236, a three car passenger train, headed by #2120, hit Train #1, headed by #1750. Don Caldwell, the fireman on #2120, was killed in the gangway as he tried to jump. "Dad" Nielson was the engineer on #2120. Nielson reported all that saved him was his watch which prevented a rod from entering his chest. Caldwell supposedly caused the wreck when he reported their orders said they should meet #1 at Spire Rock instead of at Welch. Nielson should have read the orders, however. The year before #2120 was involved in a collision with a rock near Tunnel #3 (see page 67).

JVM

The impact of the collision telescoped a coach into the baggage car. All that saved the baggageman's life was a coffin standing on end at the front of the car which kept the wreckage from coming any farther. The baggagemen reported, "The corpse came out, stood up and didn't say a damn word."

Mile post 55 is in the middle of Welch siding. The post itself is just around the corner in the 1995 photo at left. The depot and quarry switch were near the east switch. In the 1970's Burlington Northern removed the east end of the siding and left just enough of the west end to allow for setting out bad order cars or parking maintenance of way equipment. From here one can see across the big loop to Spire Rock in the distance. Spire Rock siding is just out of the picture to the right.

The 1995 photo below shows the west switch at Welch, signal masts, stubbed siding track and the telephone shack. The signal masts of the tricolor ABS signals have been vandalized and the heads removed. The photo above is taken from the rock cut in the background of this photo. While Welch looks very abandoned today, at times it was quite busy. W.R. McGee took a photo from this exact spot in 1941 showing four trains. At various times, and particularly after March 2, 1949, when Mullan Tunnel caved in, the BSL served as the main line.

Welch's Quarry Spur:

This 1908 view of Welch's Quarry shows the railroad just before it crossed the creek below the loading platform. A steam power plant can be seen in the center. The small siding was at the left and the quarry was on the hillside in the background and at right. The spur ended just below the rocky ridge seen above the west switch of the siding.

James Welch opened a granite quarry one mile off the main line at Beef Straight Creek in 1899. Welch obtained contracts to provide granite construction blocks to a variety of building sites in the Pacific Northwest, and to accommodate him, NP built a mile long spur from the main line to the quarry. In 1900 Welch siding was constructed, easing access to the spur. A mystery surrounds

Welch's Spur in that it does not appear on any NP timetables, even as an industry spur. The same was true of Parrot Spur three miles to the east. Apparently this was because of a "624 Agreement." It is not clear what this arrangement was.

The spur does appear on other NP records such as those of the engineering department. Its fate is shown in AFE 1551-25.

AFE 1551-25

Welch, Montana, Remove portion of Quarry Spur. In 1899 the Railway constructed a spur track for Mr. Jas. Welch to serve a quarry which was operating at this point. This spur was put in under old 624 agreement and the operations at this quarry have ceased for some time and the tracks are not being used beyond a point 1400 feet from the main line. Length of this spur from the head block to the end is 5419 feet and it is the joint recommendation of the Traffic and Operating Departments all of this spur with the exception of 1400 feet be taken up.

Septmber 30, 1926

Reproduced From Original Claim Map #5590

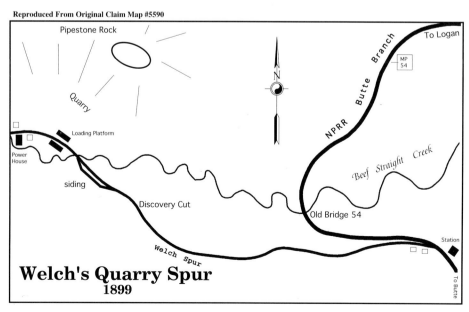

Welch's Quarry Spur
1899

The data for the map at left was taken from mining claim #5590 filed in Jefferson County by James Welch on December 20, 1899. The claim was approved by the U.S. Surveyor General on January 6, 1900. Notice that on this map Welch siding is not yet there. The siding would be at Beef Straight located at mile post 53.7 just off the map at the top. It is not clear whether "Discovery Cut" was a name for a railroad location or whether it was the original site of the mine.

Welch's quarry continued to operate until sometime after 1910. By that time, however, technology had passed it by, and concrete was replacing building stone for foundations. In addition to the structures mentioned in the newspaper articles of the day, many Welch granite curbs and paving stones were laid in Butte.

A 1908 booklet published by the University of Montana entitled *Some Economic Geology of Montana* extols the virtues of Welch granite.

The quarries near Homestake are probably the best producers. The stone is a fairly good variety of granite and is used quite extensively in the large buildings of Butte. The largest granite quarry near Butte is located at Welch's Spur, 17 miles east of Butte. The quarry is located on a spur of the main line and 1 1/2 miles from Welch's station. The granite is fairly coarse grained, however, not too coarse. The rock is black and white and does not polish well. The nodules that are found in this rock, as well as that near Helena, are much darker than the granite proper, and very fine grained.

The mass of granite forms a sort of dome, or anticline, from a side view, and breaks off when quarried, similar to the concentric decomposition of a granite boulder.

The working of this property is quite extensive for Montana. The drilling and dressing and loading is done largely by using compressed air as the power. The air is compressed on the grounds by means of steam power and has a working pressure of from 90 to 95 pounds to the square inch at the quarry. The general working force is as follows: One compressed air stone dresser, 3 hand dressers, 2 quarry men, 1 stoker, 1 blacksmith, 1 crane tender, and 1 compressed air tender.

That the quarry saw more development after 1906 is obvious when one visits the site today. The spur was extended farther up the creek. In fact the creek was diverted from its bed to allow for the extension. Rock walls were erected along the side of the rail extension so granite could be loaded at a variety of points. The shoulder of the granite dome behind the flat cars in the photo at right has been cut away, and what appears to be the foundation of a larger power plant can be found across the creek. Dressed stone steps and foundations are all that remain.

THE NEWSPAPER AND WELCH'S QUARRY

The 1906 *Anaconda Standard* ran a feature headlined "Queer Spots Around Butte" in its Sunday editions. The August 19, 1906, paper featured Welch's Quarry. Below are reproduced two photographs from that story.

NP locomotive #102 begins its 1.1 mile journey to the main line with four flatcars of Welch Quarry granite. It is passing by the siding just below the loading platform and is about to enter "Discovery Cut." The log trestle work in the foreground appears to be a device to carry the stone from the quarry to the loading platform. Beef Straight Cr. flows between the railroad and the ramp.

"Stone for the pedestal of the Daly Monument," reads the caption for this photo. The quarry is on the right, the loading platform is is in the foreground and the "town site" is along the creek. The Daly monument was being erected in Butte to commemorate Marcus Daly who died in 1900. The stone was also used in many buildings in Butte. Locomotive #102 is a NP 2-8-0 built by Baldwin.

SUNDAY MORNING, AUGUST 19. 1906   THE ANACONDA STANDARD

WELCH QUARRY HAS BEST QUALITY BUILDING STONE

Welch's Spur is located close to the Northern Pacific tracks 16 miles from Butte. From the Northern Pacific tracks, a little beyond Homestake tunnel, a spur runs up to the quarry, a distance of about one mile. Here the cars are loaded with the building stone which is now used in many places through the state, and particularly in Butte. In fact, the splendid, solid granite from Welch's spur is used almost entirely for the foundations of the many buildings now in process of erection in Butte.

The foundation stone for the marvelous excavations for the Phoenix Electric company, in the alley south of Broadway and between Main and Wyoming streets, is being supplied from this quarry. This is one of the deepest excavations ever made in the Northwest. It is to be 60 feet square and when completed will be 40 feet deep. There will be the equivalent of two stories below the street level. This depth is in order that the boilers of the company may be installed on the lowest floor, which will be 25 feet in depth. Above that, and still below the street level, will be another floor where the machinery will be installed.

The foundation stone for the viaducts now in course of construction over the Butte, Anaconda & Pacific tracks at Nevada avenue is also being supplied from the Welch quarry. The same stone is used in the foundations of many other important building operations of Butte and other cities.

The spur is a romantic spot for miles in every direction. The rockiest rocks in the Rocky mountains are to be seen, tumbled about in all kinds of fantastic shapes.

The granite at Welch's spur is the finest material for building stone to be found in the West. It much resembles the famous Quincy granite in New Hampshire. Northern Pacific engineers who have examined the quarry have declared that it would take that road 50 years of constant hauling with available equipment to haul away all the granite that is in sight at the quarries.

The owner is James Welch, who gives personal supervision to the cutting of the granite blocks and the removal of the blocks to the place where they are to be used for foundations.

Mr. Welch is the best equipped contractor in the state for all kinds of cut stone work. He is fully supplied with pneumatic tools, surfacers, rock crushers, polishers and steam derricks. One crusher is in his equipment which has a crushing capacity of 300 tons a day.

The 1900 census, however, lists far more men working at Welch's Quarry than the newspaper article above mentions to include several families with children. Most of the workers had cabins near the quarry switch at Welch siding. Some lived along the creek above the quarry.

Train operations at the quarry remain unclear. NP locomotive #102 is shown in photos hauling flat cars loaded with dressed stone. It may have been leased however, since records show Welch employed both a locomotive engineer and a fireman. Operations may have involved shunting loaded cars of granite to and from Welch siding for pick up by the local freight.

The granite quarry at Welch is shown in this 1908 photograph. The photographer is standing about at the end of the spur looking east. In the foreground are the tools for cutting and dressing the stone. In the background is the powerhouse which provided steam for the saws and hoists and compressed air for the drills. The blocks were cut from the hillside which is actually a subsidiary ridge of Pipestone Rock, seen in many railroad photographs of the area.

High School, Building Butte, Mont.

Old Butte High School at left utilized Welch granite as a foundation with brick paneling above.

The Marcus Daly statue erected in 1906 features Welch granite as its base. Originally in front of the federal court house, the statue now resides on the School of Mines campus.

The photos on this page represent three examples of structures built with Welch granite. It was considered some of the finest building stone in the Pacific Northwest -- characterized by a fine grain and black intrusions. Many of Butte's oldest buildings were constructed of it, but it was also used elsewhere. By 1920 concrete had replaced granite stones as foundation and curbing material, and asphalt had replaced cobble stones as paving material. Consequently, Welch's Quarry closed down as did several other granite quarries around Butte.

The federal court house on Main Street in Butte was constructed almost entirely of Welch granite except for brick panels between the windows. This building is still in use today.

In 1994 little remains of the quarry operation at Welch. In the foreground is the loading platform pictured on page 62. This photo looks downgrade toward the siding to the east. A dressed stone that did not make the last train remains on the platform. Others lie about the site in various states of completion. One quarry pit is on the hillside in the background. The other is behind us. Both are carved in the flank of Pipestone Rock.

The expertise of the quarry men at Welch can be seen in the building foundations that remain. The staircase at right comes down from the track level to the powerhouse located on the creek. Next to it is a stone lined dugout that perhaps served as a garage in later years. For about half a mile the creek channel has been changed and the track routed up the old creek bed. Dressed granite stones form walls on both sides of it. A dam provided a water supply for the steam boiler in the power plant. Quarry operations had quit by 1920, and the spur was removed in 1926.

Tunnel #3:

Beautiful Montana. Northern Pacific Tunnel in the Rocky Mountains.

At mile post 58.7 is Tunnel #3. This 117' unlined tunnel is the shortest on the mountain and the only one on the east side. It is #3 because the tunnels were numbered from Livingston. There were two on Bozeman Hill (Hoppers & Bozeman). This was the site of an aborted hold up attempt in 1908. The tunnel can be seen from I-90.

The 1908 Robbery Attempt:

On April 23, 1908, four men attempted to hold up the west bound NCL at Tunnel #3. Engineers Hanscomb and Gear stopped their train when they heard four torpedoes go off near tunnel #3. They were suspicious as it had been less than a year since Clow's murder two miles east near Welch.

When they alighted, they saw four men. The men lost their nerve when they saw the crew was prepared, and they fled into the rocks. The crew restarted their train, steamed to Butte and notified the sheriff.

Train master Max Kone was on the train, however, and dropped off as it started to move. He surprised Paul Felinaus and Rudolf Wenk and turned them over to Sheriff Henderson when he arrived a short time later.

Their story was they were forced to stop the train by two other men who were standing on top of the tunnel with drawn guns. Henderson searched the area and found no other tracks. He did find three sticks of dynamite, a flask of nitroglycerin and a coil of fuse.

Later two other heavily armed men were arrested in Basin, but they were found to be innocent and were released. Henderson proclaimed he felt Filinaus and Wenk were guilty and had cached their guns before Kone apprehended them. No evidence was ever found to substantiate their story, and they were later found guilty of attempted armed robbery and sent to prison.

This is R.V. Nixon's first wreck photo taken May 10, 1921. He captioned it, "In this wreck #224 with 2120 and Engineer Pete Ross hit a rock just west of the Welch tunnel. The tank of the 2120 rolled clear to the bottom of the gulch with the fireman ahead of it. But he wasn't hurt seriously. How Pete ever got out is beyond me, but he wasn't hurt." This was then inaccessible country.

WRM

Lewis Spur:

APPROACHING BUTTE, MONT. ON NORTHERN PACIFIC R. R.   77717

This 1910 postcard view shows a west bound freight about two miles below Lewis Spur near Tunnel #3. The rear helper will be cut off at Homestake, reversed on the 60' turntable and returned to Whitehall for another assignment. The retainers will need to be set for the ten mile descent into Butte. I-90 now parallels this track on the south side of the creek.

Lewis Spur was at mile post 59.1. The 1893 timetable shows it to be a single ended spur with a capacity of 20 cars. It was built at the time of the original construction to serve a wood cutting operation owned by Alderman Lewis of Butte. It remained on the 1926 profile and appears to have been removed about World War II. Little evidence of it remains today.

In 1889 a large forest fire swept the area, and the *Butte Miner* reported Alderman Lewis lost several hundred board feet of cordwood as a result. Mostly sagebrush remains today. No evidence has been found of any railroad buildings ever constructed at Lewis Spur.

This 1997 photo shows the railroad near Lewis Spur. The west bound rest area on I-90 is just below and a few hundred feet to the east of here. The spur was used to load cord wood for the mines in Butte. It was taken out about World War II. From here to the summit the railroad parallels Homestake Creek. The grade remains 2.2%.

Homestake Pit and Wye:

This 1996 view is of the east switch of Homestake at mile post 60.1. A block signal mast remains as does the Sherman & Reed taxi sign painted on the rock in the early days of passenger traffic. Many of these can still be seen. A stub entered the Homestake Pit from the east switch. Most of the fill and decomposed granite ballast on the mountain came from this pit which is now a lake. Later, the lake provided ice. Another leg was added to the spur after World War I. This served as a wye track to turn the helpers when the 60" turntable became too short.

As at Spire Rock, the carved names on the rocks at Homestake tell a story of those who lived and worked there. This stone near the east switch is one of several boulders with these marks. Records show a R.L. Daniels signed on with the NP as a road man in 1929 and worked until 1946. This may not be the same person, but the coincidence is a bit much. Other names can be seen as well.

Homestake:

JVM

Most of the railroad community of Homestake can be seen in this turn of the century photo taken from the top of Homestake Tunnel looking east. It was the most important railroad installation between Whitehall and Butte. Both a section and an order station were located here. The hand car shed and depot (a newer one would be built here after this one burns) appear in the center foreground opposite the west siding switch and industry spur. An east bound is stopped for water. The NP directed train men to water here when possible since it was company water. They had to pay for water in Butte. To the left of the depot can be seen the 60' turntable. Farther to the left are the section, bunk houses and saloon. In 1908 several boxcars were placed here to serve as homes for employees. Out of sight to the west is the Homestake ballast pit (now Homestake Lake). A wye track was built later at the pit. Homestake was the headquarters during construction. In 1956 this end of Homestake siding was moved 300 feet to the south when the tunnel was abandoned and a cut was excavated through the summit. The tunnel portals were covered, and the remaining buildings at Homestake were scheduled to be burned by the Forest Service in 1997. Even the rusty rails of the main line avoid the town site.

In 1997 the authors attempted to duplicate the photo above. Not much remains of the community at Homestake. The depot sat about where the sign is in the center. One of the dwellings remains to be burned in the distance. The tracks are now 300' to the south.

JVM

Four men lounge at the waiting room door of the 14' x 46' Homestake depot in this 1905 photograph. The section man's velocipede awaits the next call. To the rear is the section house. A train must be due because the Swift order board is showing stop. J.C. Patterson, the project engineer, had his office here during construction. The tunnel is to the west. This depot burned about 1913.

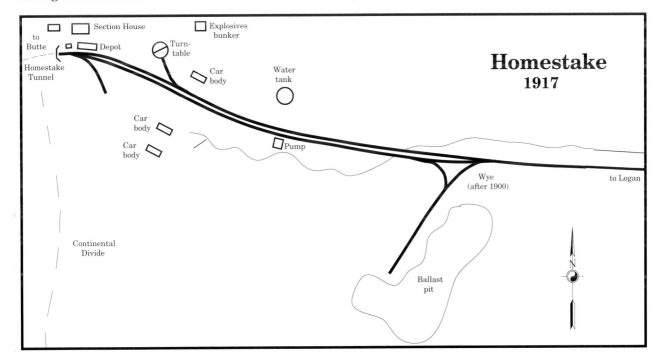

JVM

The photo above shows the second depot at Homestake. It replaced the smaller depot when it burned. It was similar to those at Willow Creek, Sappington and Cardwell. Beyond the depot is the water tank

This 1996 photo shows the cement base to the water tank on the hill overlooking Homestake. There was a wooden tank above the base. After 1908 a gasoline powered pump lifted water into the tank from a concrete lined well below the tracks. A bit to the east is Homestake Lake where the wye and ice loading facilities once were located. The tall trees around the tank show the effectiveness of fire suppression during this century. Earlier photos show a remarkable lack of trees on the east side of the pass. Homestake was the site of a large construction camp in 1889-90. Subcontractors for Keefe & Green worked on the eastern end of the tunnel from their camp here. A similar camp existed a mile to the west at Highview. The tunnel was completed in the fall of 1889, but the line was not turned over to the operating department until June 14, 1890.

JVM

In this R.V. Nixon photo taken from inside the east portal of Homestake Tunnel, one can see the "new" depot and telltale. Part of the 339' of wooden lining is also visible above the entrance. The 1902 depot, which was in the same location, burned about 1913. By the time this photo was taken in the 1950's, the bunk houses and turntable had long since been removed. The depot would be closed shortly since the new cut which bypassed the tunnel and townsite was soon to open. Many buildings were sold locally by bid, and the Homestake section house still exists in Whitehall where it was moved and turned into a private residence. The fate of the other buildings is unknown.

Homestake, at mile post 60.9, was always the major railroad installation between Whitehall and Butte. In 1889 J.C. Patterson, the Northern Pacific & Montana project engineer, had his office here. A tunnel camp of about 175 men worked on boring the tunnel westward while a similar crew worked eastward from Highview.

Homestake was the dividing point for that work supervised by Green (east side) and that supervised by Keefe (west side). Workers, primarily Italians, existed in primitive tents and "wickiups."

E.H. McHenry located the route during the winter of 1888/89. Most expected the line to be built via Pipestone Pass seven miles to the south. McHenry, however, discovered the Homestake route was seven miles shorter and forty feet lower than Pipestone. The Milwaukee Road later utiliz-

ed Pipestone. In its prime about 40 railroad employees were stationed at Homestake.

In 1902 a 14' x 46' depot and a 15' x 20' freight house were erected. A 60' plate girder turntable for turning the helpers was already in place. In 1907 an ice house and two bunkhouses were built. Another bunkhouse was added in 1909 as well as a tool house and section house.

The water system went through a major upgrade in 1908. The company built a wooden tank 30' in diameter on a concrete base on the hill overlooking the town site and set an 11' x 11' x 9' cement well in the creek bottom. A gas powered pump and a 14' x 20' pump house were erected along the south side of the passing track across from the tank. When the depot burned about 1913, a new, modern depot was constructed,

similar in design to those at Cardwell, Sappington and Willow Creek.

Homestake served as an order station. Most trains working up the 2.2% grade on either side of the mountain required helpers. In the early days these helpers were turned on the turntable at Homestake and returned light to either Butte or Whitehall. When steam engines became too large for the 60' turntable (after about 1900), a wye track was built as part of the Homestake Pit lead at the east end of the siding. The pit provided most of the decomposed granite that was used as ballast on the hill. Later a flume was constructed to make a lake of the old pit, and in winter it provided ice for the system. In 1907 an ice loading platform, boiler house and elevator were installed to support this effort.

Homestake Tunnel (Tunnel #4):

JVM

The photo above shows the east portal of the Homestake Tunnel (#4) and the west switch at Homestake. The 706' tunnel, which was wood lined for 339', cuts through the summit of the continental divide at an elevation of 6,328.' The mid-point of the tunnel was the summit. The wooden telltale at the entrance warned brakemen on top of the cars of low clearance ahead.

JVM

NP locomotive #1213 prepares to enter the east portal of Homestake Tunnel pushing a string of flat cars with track equipment and men on board in this undated photo.

12618. Continental Divide, Butte, Mont.

A wooden sign marks the summit of the continental divide above the west tunnel approach at Highview in this early postcard view. It indicates Pacific Slope to the left and Atlantic Slope to the right. The "Red's Boots" sign on the rock is typical of early billboards in the area.

Rails were laid through Homestake Tunnel in January, 1890, six months before the BSL was turned over to the operating department. Approximately 300 men had worked six months to drive the 706' long bore. It was wooden lined for 339.' It remainedbasiclly unchanged throughout its 66 years of service.

The station at the west portal would later be named Highview, and it would spring into prominence during the statehood elections of 1889 as the site of a notorious election scandal. F.J. Haynes, the widely known Northern Pacific photographer, shot several views from Highview during his trip over the line in 1893.

Passengers on the left side of west bound trains exiting the tunnel were treated to a magnificent view of the Silver Bow Valley and Butte in the distance as they made the corner at Highview. While only ten miles from the city, the trains dropped 749' in elevation on the 2.2% grade.

This R.V. Nixon photo, taken from the east switch at Highview, shows the west portal of Homestake Tunnel. When the tunnel was bypassed in 1956, both portals were collapsed leaving very little of this scene visible today. The railroad numbered tunnels from Livingston, hence Homestake Tunnel's #4 designation. The hill above the tunnel is the summit of the continental divide.

JVM

6. The West Side: Highview to Butte

Highview:

The Butte Short Line was built in two segments. It was decided that Keefe would oversee the ten miles of construction from Butte to the tunnel. Since some preliminary grade work had been done through Jefferson Canyon by the U&N between mile posts 30 and 35, they felt Green's segment would be the easier. This did not turn out to be true.

Keefe supervised his work from his camp at Highview. Drum & Breckenridge subcontracted the remainder to Butte. One thousand Italian laborers worked west of Highview. Railroad facilities at Highview were primitive, and soon after the opening of the line virtually all structures were removed including the notorious "house with the paper over the windows."

During construction in 1890, a car broke loose at the tunnel and ran clear to the Montana Union depot in Butte before stopping. Luckily no one was injured. While operations on the mountain seem to have been relatively accident free, incidents such as this this were not unknown.

The postcard view at right is on the 1902 grade approaching tunnel #5. Generations of photographers have been impressed with the rocky beauty around Highview.

SUMMIT OF THE ROCKIES, NEARING BUTTE ON THE N. P. R. R.

No. 88

This 1910 postcard view looks west from High view. It shows the revised alignment leading to Tunnel #5 which was completed in 1902. The original grade swung left here and crossed two wooden bridges before rejoining the present route just west of the tunnel.

Nearing Butte on the Northern Pacific, 40.

NEARING BUTTE ON THE NORTHERN PACIFIC.   39

The postcard view at left looks east, back through the same rocky cut shown in the postcard on the previous page. Highview is just around the corner out of sight.

WORK TRAIN IN COLLISION

COME TOGETHER ON GRADE
WITH A TERRIFIC CRASH

BUTTE, Dec. 29 -- Two work trains on the Northern Pacific tracks met in a head on collision about a quarter of a mile this side of Homestake tunnel about 11 o'clock yesterday morning and that a number of men were not killed or seriously injured appears almost miraculous. Three engines were more or less damaged, a caboose containing eight men was telescoped and flat cars were damaged. Traffic was delayed for almost five hours.

The trains which collided were at work on the track, filling in and doing other repair and grade work. Such trains travel on orders regarding the movements of regular passenger and freight trains, but it is understood that they have not means of knowing of the movements of each other. The result was that when a work train consisting of several dirt cars and two engines reached a sharp curve this side of the tunnel on the down grade, there was no warning of the approach of a second train, climbing the hill and consisting of an engine, a flat car and a caboose.

When they were several feet apart, the engineers and firemen applied brakes and reversed and then jumped. The train on the downgrade, being much heavier, raised havoc with the lighter train.

Montana Weekly Record   Dec. 31, 1903

Burlington Northern's sign marks the summit of Homestake Pass at the old site of Highview. The new summit is one half mile west. In 1956 Highview was reduced to a single ended spur. Nothing remains of the construction camp which housed about 200 Italian tunnel workers.

Precinct 34 (Highview):

The workers at the construction camp at Highview played an interesting political role as Montana statehood was achieved in 1889. Montanans voted on their new constitution in October of that year. The events are thoroughly mixed up with the developing feud between Marcus Daly and William Clark that erupted into what would become known as "the war of the Copper Kings."

Silver Bow County traditionally voted Democratic. Daly and Clark were part of the powerful Democratic political machine in Butte and Missoula. In the election of 1888, Clark ran as the Democratic candidate for the US Senate from the Territory of Montana. But he and Daly had a falling out resulting in a feud that would be fought on many battlefields.

To simplify a complicated story, Daly decided it was better for his financial interests if a Republican candidate won the senatorial election. Consequently, Daly switched parties and brought his business and political power to bear. He succeeded in getting the Republican candidate Carter elected for which Clark never forgave him. Shortly thereafter, Daly returned to the Democratic fold, but the feud continued, resulting in a split in the Democratic party that would continue for years. These events resulted in the new state going Republican in 1889 and a political scandal at Highview.

M.H. Keefe of Keefe & Green had established a tunnel construction camp of about 170 men at Highview. Keefe, a Democrat, took the crew to Butte prior to the October elections and registered them to vote although many were Italian immigrants who could not speak English. There were so many registered voters at Highview, a precinct was established known as Precinct 34.

Election day was October 31, 1889. One hundred seventy-four votes were cast at Precinct 34. Democratic candidates consistently received 171 votes, and Republican candidates consistently received three. When the returns were announced, people became suspicious.

It was soon learned that the actual counting of the Precinct 34 votes had been done inside a building at Highview with no one but the election judges present. The judges had pasted paper over the windows to keep curious onlookers from watching.

When the Precinct 34 votes were canvassed by the county commissioners, other irregularities were discovered. The law required that the names of voters be kept in a book in the order in which they voted. At Highview workers appeared to have voted in alphabetical order. Republicans charged that everyone at Highview was told they either needed to vote Democratic or lose their jobs. A number of Highview residents testified that they had voted Republican and their votes were not reflected in the totals.

As a result the county commissioners rejected the returns from Precinct 34 on the basis of election fraud. The Silver Bow County clerk, however, was a Democrat, and he refused to send the ammended returns to the state.

After numerous maneuvers, the State Board of Canvassers decided to count all of the Silver Bow precincts except Precinct 34. With the loss of those 171 Democratic votes, the entire Republican slate from Silver Bow County was certified as elected. Had they been seated, it would have given the Republicans a majority.

The Silver Bow County Democratic central committee applied to the judge of the second judicial district for a writ of *mandamus* to compel the county to count the votes from the disputed precinct.

Legal wrangling followed, and the issue became, "Did the canvassing board have the right to reject the returns because they believed fraud had been committed? Or was the duty of a canvassing board limited to checking and tabulating the vote as found in the returns of the precinct officers?" Republicans brought forward witnesses who said they had voted Republican and their votes had not been counted. Democrats countered with affidavits from the same seven men who swore they had been bribed to vote Republican.

Judge Stephen DeWolf issued his decision on November 7, 1889. He ruled that the county board of canvassers was strictly an administrative body and had no power to reject returns. He then ordered the Silver Bow County commissioners to count the votes from Precinct 34 since fraud had not been proven. The Silver Bow County clerk then issued certificates of election to the five Democratic candidates and declared invalid the five certificates of election for the Republican candidates.

When the issue reached Helena, it was found that two seperate groups considered themselves elected as representatives. Only the Republican body was recognized. The Democratic body was never seated.

Highview, it had turned out, had played a pivotal role in the makeup of the first legislative assembly, and newspapers of the day made constant reference to the "scandal at Precinct 34" or to "that ignominious house with the paper over the windows." They took sides depending on their political leanings--a sampling of which is included on the adjoining page.

THERE WERE NO FRAUDS

A Man Who Knows Tells of the Election at Tunnel Precinct

One of the voters who cast his ballot at the Tunnel precinct in the late election was in the city yesterday. Reference is made to John McEvoy. He has been a resident of Montana for twenty-three years, and in his time has done a goodly share in the work of railroad construction in the territory. At present, Mr. McEvoy is a foreman under Keefe & Gallagher, sub contractors for Keefe, Green & Barbour, general contractors for the Northern Pacific road. His gang is only one of eleven gangs engaged in railroad work, and his scene of operations is two miles this side of the tunnel. When asked what he knew about the allegations that there was fraud practiced at the Tunnel polling place Mr. McEvoy said:

"Only four of the sixty men in my camp wanted to vote and only that four left their work to do so. The others are Italian and only one of them had a vote, and he would not leave his work. The four men who did go to the polls were docked a half day each for lost time. I took half a day off to go to the polls and lost a half day's pay in consequence. I know that all the men who lost time by registering themselves were charged for that time, and that all those who lost time in voting were charged for that, too.

I was at the polls a long time during the day and asked many of the voters what ticket they had cast. In every instance the reply was 'Straight,' and when I asked 'Straight what?' they replied that their tickets had been cast straight for the Democratic candidates. I told some of them jokingly after they had voted, that they were good for their time and pointed out to them that Mr. Keefe of the firm Keefe, Green & Barbour -- and who by the way is related neither in blood nor business to Mr. Keefe of Keefe & Gallagher -- was a black Republican and a candidate in Lewis and Clark county. The men replied that Mr. Keefe might be their boss in business, but he could not control their votes.

I know that there was not an attempt made to influence the vote in any man who voted that day. Having been railroad contracting so long in this part of the country, I know hundreds of laboring men engaged on the work. I met scores that I knew at the polls that day and I have seen them since and I know that they are mad at the thought of being disenfranchised. I could get more than a hundred to stop work and lose a day's pay for the chance of coming here to testify how they voted -- to swear in their votes.

All of the men who voted at the tunnel are intelligent men. They need no instruction as to how to prepare their ballots, and certainly they knew for whom they wanted to vote. Furthermore, they are qualified voters. I am satisfied that the Democratic majority there was due as much to McGinnis's [a Democratic candidate] popularity as anything else. The men knew of him as a man who had done a great deal for the territory and who would do more if he was elected.

We hate to be cheated out of our votes. The men are all eager to be given a chance to tell under oath for whom they voted. They are willing to tell, and their statements would settle the whole controversy. Keefe and Gallagher have volunteered to stop work long enough to enable the men to come here and testify, and will use their teams to bring them here. I hope that the offer may be accepted."

Mr. McEvoy had come up especially on an errand from the disenfranchised working men to see if they could not go in a body before a justice of the peace and make affidavit to the votes they cast, or in some way assert their rights as American freemen.

Butte Daily Miner   October 18, 1889

OFFICIAL RETURN, INCLUDING THE 34TH PRECINCT

34th Precinct labeled - Camp No.1, Butte & Gallatin Railroad

For Constitution	172	Against Constitution	2
(D) Maginnis	171	(R) Carter	3
(D) Toole	171	(R) Power	3
(D) Conrad	171	(R) Rickards	3
(D) Sec of State	171	(R) Sec of State	3
(D) Atty General	169	(R) Atty General	5
(D) Treasurer	172	(R) Treasurer	2
(D) Sheriff	165	(R) Sheriff	9

It is expected that objections will be raised in the case of the Tunnel precinct.... At Meaderville Republicans handed out tickets saying, "I cannot read, write or speak English. I want the Republican judge to make out a straight Republican ticket."

Butte Weekly Miner Oct. 16, 1889

To have the will of the majority of the people subverted by a gang of imported Italian graders who are here only while the railroad is building, and who are in no proper sense qualified voters, is an indefensible contravention of the clear meanng of the law.

Inter Mountain   Oct. 8, 1889

"*The judges locked the doors, nailed paper over the windows, excluded the clerk and denied admittance to any and all persons from the polling place.*"

Affidavit of   William O'Reagan

THE EFFECT OF THE JUDGMENT

We have heretofore presented at some length the evil consequences following the great crime perpetrated by the canvassing board of Silver Bow county in its attempt to throw out precinct No. 34, defeat the voice of the people, and prevent the legitimate results of the election. We have seen that all fair minded men, regardless of party affinities, condemn in unmeasured terms the willful usurpation of power by Hall and Jack [county board of canvass] and the betrayal of the trust confided to them, in their unscrupulous effort to serve political aspirants to senatorial honors....

Daily Independent   Jan. 3, 1890

Highview Tunnel (Tunnel #5):

Highview Tunnel (#5) is located at mile post 61.7. It is 628' long, and the eastern third is lined with timber. It was not part of the original construction. It was completed in 1902 during the general upgrade of the line that saw wooden trestles filled in or replaced with steel. The only actual line relocation, however, happened just east of Highview.

Originally, the grade passed around a boulder strewn ridge over two large wooden bridges and through a deep, rocky cut. The F.J. Haynes photo on page 21, taken in 1893, is of the eastern most of the two bridges.

Rather than replace them with steel (they were too large), the NP decided to avoid them altogether by driving a new tunnel through the ridge and relocating one half mile of line. The project was completed in 1902.

The rocky cut of the original line can still be seen just above the interstate west of the summit at Homestake. Only rotten timbers of the bridges remain strewn in the gulch bottoms.

Ironically, when the Homestake Tunnel was abandoned and the line relocated in 1956 to its present location, the overburden from the daylighted summit cut was taken to provide a new grade across the gulch spanned by the eastern wooden bridge of the original alignment. The plan was to ease the rocky corner west of Highview and eliminate Tunnel #5 by returning to the original grade via the filled-in gulch. The realignment was not finished before the BSL was abandoned. The massive fill can still be seen just west of the summit.

Tunnel #5 is in poor shape. The wooden liner has rotted, and several roof supports have collapsed. Before the route could ever be reopened the tunnel would either need to be relined or the new grade would have to be finished.

The west portal of Highview Tunnel basks in the late afternoon sun in this 1995 photo. The wooden liner on the eastern end has suffered the ravages of time. Only ATV's use the tunnel now. The original alignment went right, out around the ridge and over two large wooden bridges which have long since disappeared.

Obviously, Sherman & Reed in Butte was a diversified operation. The advertisement on the rock near Highview also lists "Livery" and "Undertaking" as specialities of the firm. One would not think many passengers on the NCL would be interested in a funeral, but one can never tell.

North Coast Limited

Cliffs on N. P. R. R. near Butte, Mont. 11.

A west bound passenger train descends the west side of Homestake Pass near Highview in this 1908 postcard view. The train's helper probably cut off at Homestake about two miles east of here. Butte is still eight miles ahead down a long stretch of 2.2% grade.

The spectacular scenery along the Butte Short Line led to many excursions. In this undated postcard view, several young ladies pose dramatically on one of the innumerable huge boulders near Highview. It is impossible to tell whether they hiked up, dropped off a local train, or perhaps were brought up on the hand car of a young section hand. All three were common in the early days. The smog from the smelters in Butte was so bad that any excuse would serve to get out of town. The mine owners themselves sponsored weekends away for their employees. The Northern Pacific ran specials to Pipestone Springs over the BSL as well as to other locations. These trips became very popular. Nothing much has changed over the years. This portion of the Homestake route is still a popular recreation site with ATV riders, mountain bike riders and hikers.

Bridge 63:

This 1995 view of bridge 63 looks west toward Butte. The bridge is curved and superelevated toward the valley floor. The author can remember the spectacular sensation of being in the vista dome as the NCL crossed the bridge. The feeling was one of being airborn as he looked straight down into the gulch.

Bridge #63 crosses Ealean Gulch at mile post 63.8. Like its two counterparts on the east side it was originally wooden. As part of the general upgrade of the line that began in 1900, it was rebuilt out of steel in 1902. The 601' bridge is on a 12 degree corner and is the longest bridge on the Butte Short Line. It has four 60', one 30', seven 40', and one 50' deck plate girder spans. The concrete abutment on the west end bears the date 1902 inscribed near the top.

Bridge 63 can be seen easily from the valley, and it is the most noteworthy feature on the west side of the pass. It always provided passengers a thrill because of its superelevation. In later years, it was not uncommon for passengers in the vista dome to gasp as the car appeared to swing out into space as the North Coast Limited passed over the span.

A story in the May 28, 1903, *Anaconda Standard* tells of a tragic accident near the bridge that took the lives of two Northern Pacific employees. A work train was coming downgrade through a four mile per hour speed restriction after spreading ballast. A young engineer by the name of McCarrey was at the throttle.

Through inexperienced handling, the train gathered speed to 20 miles per hour, and seven cars derailed on a sharp curve near Bridge 63. Machinist John V. Logan and switchman John O'Mara were killed instantly "by the derailment of the train on the air line." O'Mara was married, but luckily had no children. Unfortunately, this kind of accident happened on occasions.

Today Bridge 63 has an almost unfinished look. Apparently the end of service caught it in mid-upgrade, and set outs were never completed. The bridge ties are of uneven length on the uphill side as though they were never trimmed after installation. As with Bridges 51 and 52, no hand railing or walkway is present. The view of the Silver Bow Valley from Bridge 63 is spectacular. A rock slide near the west end, however, has blocked the tracks to any track vehicles.

Engineer Frank Clow mentioned in the Missoulian story at right is the same engineer killed in 1907 at the hands of bandits at Welch. To what degree his experience in 1903 contributed to his actions in 1907 is unclear.

The 1903 Holdup Near Skones:

SUSPECT ARRESTED AT BUTTE BELIEVED TO BE A TRAIN ROBBER

William McCullagh Name of Man and Circumstantial Evidence Is Strong Against Him

Particulars of the Burlington Holdup Which Occurred Near Butte

Bell Slightly Wounded

Railroad Offers $5,000 Reward

Special to The Missoulian.

Butte, Feb. 12 -- The holdup of the Burlington express yesterday morning near Homestake is one of the most daring on record. Two men boarded the train and dynamited the safe, securing something over $400. Mail Clerk W.M. Bell of Billings was shot in an encounter but not seriously wounded. The desperadoes made good their getaway and now the officers are on their track with blood hounds. William McCullagh was arrested on suspicion today for being connected with the holdup. The Northern Pacific, through Superintendent Boyle of Livingston, has offered a reward of $5,000 for the capture of the bandits.

Conductor G.C. Hotrum had charge of the train which left Butte at 12:01. Engineer Frank Clow and helper were on engine 61 and Engineer Angus McArthur had charge of the second engine. When the train came to a standstill, the robbers compelled the fireman of 61 to uncouple the cars between the baggage car and smoker. Then they compelled the other engine to move the baggage coach, mail car and express car away about 800 feet.

Mail Clerk W.M. Bell was compelled to leave the postal car on threat of having his car blown up. The fireman was forced to dynamite the express car and set off the dynamite on top of the through safe. Several shots were fired before the cars were uncoupled and one or two shots after the head end of the train had been moved to a point where the express car was dynamited. Engineer McArthur narrowly escaped being shot just before he brought his train to a stop. His overcoat hanging on a hook in the cab behind him contained the bullet evidently intended for him, which was fired at

by the robber. Mail Clerk Bell, while on the ground, was also grazed by a bullet in the fleshy part of the hip. The dynamite which the fireman was given to use was evidently wet and Mail Clerk Bell smiled at the futile efforts being made to set it off when one of the robbers happened to see him and hit him with butt end of his gun over the eye.

Superintendent Boyle and Trainmaster Ott were on the rear of the train number six in the division superintendent's car 1450, freight train 56 followed number six out of Butte and Trainmaster Ott, as soon as it was apparent that there was a holdup, flagged the freight train and took the rear engine helper off this freight train and started for Butte.

This move was noted by the robbers and they immediately desisted in their efforts to break open the large safe in the express car, contenting themselves with taking what money they found in the small way express safe, which is said to amount to about $400.

They disappeared among the rocks and a little later showed up on the flat below the train a half mile away. They were followed down the mountain to within two miles of Butte where they disappeared near the race track. Officers with Conley and McTague's bloodhounds in charge of their keeper, Joe Queensberry, were brought from Deer Lodge to Butte on train number two, arriving there at 4:50 am.

The first arrest in the train robbery case took place this afternoon when Detective Murphy took into custody a large, heavy-set man, about 33 years old, who gave his name as William McCullagh, and said he came from California about two weeks ago to get married.

McCullagh was arrested in the Montana saloon about 2:30 o'clock. He had on his person a belt containing $485, and he said that he

brought the money with him from California.

There are two suspicious circumstances connected with McCullagh's alleged conduct and the money found on him. In an express package said to have been secured by the train robbers there were two $100 bills, according to the police, and in McCullagh's belt were seven $5 and one $100 bill.

Detective Murphy also stated that he was told by a man whose name he did not give that some time in the early hours this morning McCullagh tried to get a $100 bill changed in a saloon. The man also told Murphy that he saw a big pistol in the arrested man's possession. He was sure of one gun, and thought the man may have had two.

When arrested McCullagh denied that he had tried to change the bill named, but after had been lodged in jail he admitted changing a $50 bill. The change in his possession amounted to $39.50. His room was searched after his arrest, but nothing incriminating was found. The man did not give the name of the woman he said he came to marry.

Sheriff Quinn of Butte, who scoured the flat and the hills surrounding the place of the robbery for a radius of three or four miles for hours after it occurred, found distinct footprints of the two robbers in the snow, and also tracks of their buggy, and a mask one of them wore and cartridges from a 30-30 rifle and two pistols, a 38 and a 44. From the marks they left behind them the moves they made after they left town and reached the place of the holdup and the course they took afterward were made plain in the estimation of most of the officers who visited the scene.

Missoulian   **February 13, 1903**

Skones (Adams):

SUMMIT OF THE ROCKIES, NEARING BUTTE ON THE N. P. R. R.

The 3,130' Skones siding at mile post 65.5 was not built until the line was upgraded in 1900-1902. Only five miles from Butte, it was probably put in to allow for the cooling of brakes and wheels on west bound trains. In the days of retainers and wooden cars, this was necessary or friction fires would result.

Most of the siding is on the last of thirteen 12 degree curves on the Homestake route. Skones siding crosses Maude S Creek. The speculation is that Skones is the sight of the Italian laborers' camp burned during the construction of the grade in 1889. The Italian camp was supposedly on "Dead Woman's Creek" which does not show on any current maps of the area.

No record has been found of any railroad structures at Skones other than a telephone booth in later years. The 1903 hold up covered on the previous page took place between Skones and Bridge 63 as did the 1903 runaway.

Like Welch, most of Skones siding was removed in the 1970's. Only two hundred feet or so of the east end remain as a stub. Today young quaking aspen trees obscure most of the remaining track.

This 1910 postcard view looks east up the 2.2% grade between Skones and Bridge 63. Today a boulder weighing several hundred pounds lies between the rails in the cut in this photo. It was near here that the 1903 robbery took place.

This 1995 photo looks upgrade at the east switch at Skones. For a short time this was called Adams. Only a few feet of track remain of the 3,130' siding. The remainder was taken up in the 1970's. Burlington Northern and vandals have taken or shot out most of the parts from the three color ABS block signals which served as the home signals at Skones. The summit at Homestake is five miles east, and Butte is five miles west.

Butte:

Butte's history does not begin with the railroads. The railroads came to Butte because by 1890 it had become a major revenue producing and political center for their western operations. In just 35 years Butte had become the focus of railroad interest.

In 1856 a small group of prospectors discovered a brown colored upthrust of rock on the shoulder of "Big Butte." Someone, perhaps an Indian, had dug a trench with an elk antler lying nearby. This discovery marked the beginning of the development of Butte and the mining district surrounding it.

In 1864 a party of miners found gold near a bend of the creek just west of Big Butte. They named the creek "Silver Bow" because, in the light of the setting sun, the glistening water at the bend in the creek reminded them of an Indian's bow. A small gold rush followed, and by 1867, 300-350 miners had filed claims along Silver Bow Creek. By 1869 the placer claims had been mostly worked out. Some quartz bearing properties were located below Big Butte, however, and Butte City began to grow along the flanks of the outcrop.

The complex nature of Butte's ore, an amalgam of silver, copper, manganese, zinc and lead, stumped early millers. Their technology could not easily separate the gold and silver from the "waste" metals. Yet Butte enjoyed some success throughout the 1870's as a silver camp, but the 1873 panic drove down prices, and many of the mines came up for sale. Despite this setback, by the middle of the decade, Butte had 1,000 inhabitants.

Shrewd investors recognized Butte's potential and began buying up some of the richer claims cheaply. Ownership of the mines passed from the hands of the original pioneers to the hands of financiers. They brought with them the capitol and technology to develop the claims.

These early financiers included Samuel T. Hauser of Helena (who later was prominent in building NP branch lines), William Andrews Clark of Deer Lodge and the Walker Brothers of Salt Lake City. The latter brought mining engineer Marcus Daly to Butte to investigate their recently purchased Alice property. Daly's survey of the Alice Mine convinced him that Butte's future lay not in silver but in copper. In fact the silver bearing ore was about played out, but excavations uncovered huge quantities of copper. Daly and Clark each developed new smelting technology which made refining the ore economically feasible. The rest is history.

1552. The Richest Hill in the World, Butte, Montana. On Oregon Short Line R. R.

An Oregon Short Line postcard shows mines in Walkerville near Butte.

A page taken from an 1890's Northern Pacific guide book shows some of the early Butte mines including the Marcus Daly's Anaconda.

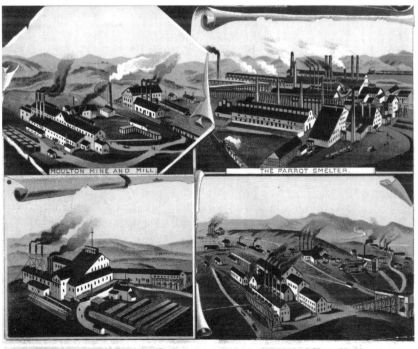

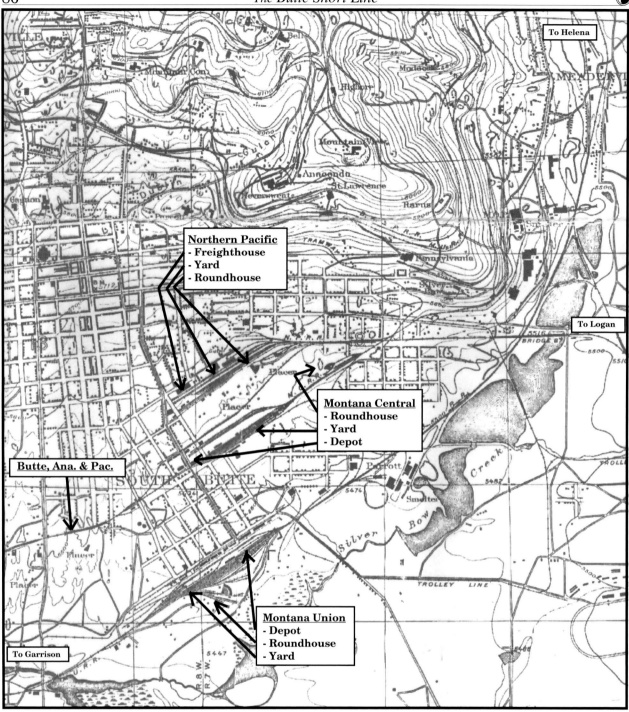

Northern Pacific
- Freighthouse
- Yard
- Roundhouse

Montana Central
- Roundhouse
- Yard
- Depot

Butte, Ana. & Pac.

Montana Union
- Depot
- Roundhouse
- Yard

To Helena

To Logan

To Garrison

The Butte map above has been reproduced from an 1895 United States Geological Survey map. The map bases Butte's elevation of 5,516' above sea level on the Northern Pacific's bridge crossing Silver Bow Creek. The lease on the Montana Union line to Garrison will not be the NP's for another year. While NP passenger trains are using the MU depot, the freight yard and roundhouse are located farther up on the hill, east of Arizona Street just north of the Montana Central complex. After 1896 more and more of the NP operations will move to the MU site. The new NP -UP Union Depot will be built in 1905 on the site of the MU depot.

The map reflects the new Butte, Anaconda & Pacific tracks in Butte which were completed in 1892. BA&P tracks will soon replace MU tracks on much of Butte Hill. The Milwaukee Road will arrive in 1908.

Butte
1895

This undated Northern Pacific postcard identifies Butte as the "Richest Hill on Earth," a popular advertising theme. The tracks in the foreground belong to the Butte, Anaconda & Pacific. Most of the hill pictured in the back ground disappeared into the Berkley Pit which the Anaconda Copper Company opened in the 1950's.

SECTION OF THE "RICHEST HILL IN THE WORLD," BUTTE, MONT.

Along the Scenic Highway: Through the Land of Fortune

Butte is unique among the cities of the world. It takes its name from a large, isolated butte in the western part of the city. Possessing all the untold wealth of its tremendous copper deposits, with thousands of well paid miners,

Butte

Population: 39,165
Altitude: 5490 ft.

with a large and growing trade in commercial lines, it is an odd and interesting combination of frontier mining camp and modern city, smoke-begrimed manufacturing point and orderly and well kept residential center. It is a city of glaring, violent contrasts, when money seems quite the easiest of all things to obtain, where men work furiously and spend the proceeds of their labor with open hand, where the finer instincts of modern city life struggle constantly with the old order of things, and when the mining camp and twentieth century municipality have been mixed into one ragged and gnarled mass, but have not yet quite blended. Butte boasts with reason that it is the greatest mining camp in the world, and may, with equal reason, boast of its achievements as a modern city. It has a fine library, and Columbia Gardens, in the suburbs, is a most interesting park, owned by private interests. Butte possesses good hotels and business blocks, paved streets, and all the usual improvements found in older cities, and almost under the shadow of the tall smoke stacks of her great mines stand homes in which the comforts and luxuries of life have been wrought out to their finest manifestations. The mines of Butte top her every hill and are indicated by the great shaft hoists and smoke stacks piercing the sky line and marking where in the depths of the earth, the marvelously rich copper veins lie. Day and night, without cessation, the year round, the miners delve and toil in these shafts and cross cuts, sending ton after ton of the valuable gray ore to the surface to be quickly transferred to the smelters and there reduced to merchantable metal. The Butte mines have produced approximately $800,000,000, of which sixty per cent has come from copper. It produces 30% of the copper mined in the United States.

Butte, seen at night, with its thousands of dancing electric lights and the glare of fire from its huge smelters, presents a sight one will never forget.

The small stream known at Butte as the Silver Bow River is followed by the railway and becomes successively the Deer Lodge, Hell Gate, Missoula, and Clark fork of the Columbia before it flows into Lake Pend d'Oreille, in Idaho.

 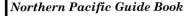

By 1906, however, the day of the individual "Copper King" was over, and most of the holdings on the hill were being operated by the Amalgamated Copper Co. This later became the Anaconda Copper Co., named after Daly's original mine.

As early as 1890, one fifth of the state's population lived within sight of Butte. What had started out as a struggling silver camp had by 1914 grown to a city numbering almost 40,000 people. The mines provided the majority of the world's copper, and Butte had become the largest city between Minneapolis and Seattle. Despite its cosmopolitan aspects, Butte never quite shook its mining town image, a legacy that lingers to this day.

By 1910 five railroads served the Butte. The Union Pacific and the Great Northern both reached it via lengthy branch lines, yet in that year traffic from Butte and Anaconda accounted for 10% of the total traffic on the UP.

The Northern Pacific served Butte via a secondary main line, yet its crack passenger train, the North Coast Limited, passed through Butte rather than Helena

The Butte, Anaconda & Pacific connected the "Mining City" and the "Smelter City" on a heavily built line which by 1914 was electrified and being looked at as a model by other western roads such as the GN and the Milwaukee.

Finally, the Milwaukee Road, which at the time of its construction in 1907-09 was connected at the corporate level with the Anaconda Company, crossed the continental divide over Pipestone Pass, following the Ray survey, funded by the Butte Board of Trade 20 years earlier and rejected by the Northern Pacific. It made the Milwaukee the only one of the five railroads serving the city to actually place Butte on its main line despite Butte's volume of traffic.

Northern Pacific R. R. Station, BUTTE, Mont.

George S. Johnson & Sons of Chicago built the new Union Depot in Butte on the site of the former Montana Union structure. The $100,000 contract was announced in May, 1905, and the building was completed by the end of the year. The postcard view above was mailed in 1914 but is taken from an earlier image.   WMM

This interior view shows the two story waiting room. Signs over the doors on the balcony indicate offices for the yard master and car foreman. The women's lounge is the first door left of the arrival board.

Above is a street view of the Butte depot. It sits at the south end of Arizona St. in an area known originally as South Butte. It was served by electric streetcars until 1939.

A DISASTEROUS WRECK

A Northern Pacific Freight Telescopes the Through Sleeper Yesterday Afternoon

Instantly Killing Hon. H.W. Lord of Devil's Lake, Dakota, and Seriously Injuring Eight Others.

The Northern Pacific was the scene of another accident yesterday which cost one estimable man his life and seriously injured eight others. Through the inexcusable carelessness of someone the loop train from the east was left standing on the main track near the "Y" just east of the city until a heavy freight train plunged into it with the result as stated. The names of the killed and injured were as follows:

Henry W. Lord of Devil's Lake, Dakota, killed instantly while escaping from the sleeper.

S.B. Calderhead of Butte, injured seriously about the back and head.

Mrs. S.B. Calderhead, injured in the head, shoulder and knee.

John R. Coterell of Dayton, O., injured about head and legs.

Mrs. John R. Coterell, bruised about the breast and shoulders.

Mrs. Allan F. Cook, two wounds in the forehead.

Timothy Donohue, engineer, left leg broken in jumping.

Charles Reed, fireman, ankle sprained.

Daniel M. Lourey, engineer, face cut and scratched and foot turned.

THE ACCIDENT

It is the custom of the Northern Pacific to drop the through sleeper at the "Y" where it is taken up by the Montana Union and pulled to Garrison to connect with the main line. This was done yesterday afternoon, the car at that time containing some 10 or 12 passengers. The train then ran down to the depot, arriving on time, 1:55 o'clock. About 12 minutes after the regular Livingston freight, a double header under charge of Conductor Oliver, pulled out, thinking the track was clear. For some reason the Montana Union switch engine was slow in getting around after the doomed sleeper, and just as they were in the act of coupling on to pull it out of the way the men were horrified to see the heavy freight train bearing down upon them from the long trestle across the run. Their first attempt

at coupling failed, and finding that no time was left for a second effort the engine was wisely backed out of the way and the men undertook to warn the inmates of the car of their peril.

IN THE CAR

As soon as the meaning of their cries was understood there was a wild rush from the inside, everyone attempting to get out by the nearest door. In the smoker at the south end of the car were the porter and three passengers, among them the unfortunate Mr. Lord. They all ran out upon the vestibule and sprang down upon the track, a move that proved fortunate for all save Mr. Lord. He was a little lame and reached the ties just in time to be caught by the car as it surged forward under the powerful impetus of those two engines backed by twelve heavily loaded cars. In an instant he was under the wheels and in another instant he had been crushed by the shattered locomotive and thrown on one side, literally cut in pieces.... Mr. Coterell was thrown violently to the floor with his wife and Mrs. Calderhead upon him. None of them were dangerously injured....

Inter Mountain   **January 28, 1891**

This 1995 photo of the Butte Union Depot show s it boarded up and abandoned. An engineering firm has remodeled the former restaurant into an office complex, but the depot itself and the freight house are in sad repair. The Montana Western has leased Butte Yard from Burlington Northern as well as the Butte to Garrison line. Its operations do not extend beyond mile post 68 on the former BSL.

Switch engine #982 in Butte Yard, October 27, 1906. From left to right: Engineer Cauley, Brakeman G.B. Noll, Fireman Palmer, Helper Grant, Helper Clark, Foreman Gostard.

PHP

Warehouse Explosion - January 15, 1895

About 10 PM January 15, 1895, a fire was discovered in a warehouse full of flour next to the NP freight house complex in Butte. The fire spread rapidly, and soon the entire building was involved, lighting up the sky. Before the fire department could respond, the fire jumped to the Kenyon, Connell Commercial Company which sold commercial hardware. Soon hundreds of Butte residents had turned out to watch the fire.

Few knew the hardware warehouse held 350 boxes of dynamite contrary to the city ordinance which prohibited the warehousing of explosives within the city limits. As the fireman began to battle the fire, one small explosion went off. Some bystanders began to retreat, but before they could get away a huge explosion ripped the warehouse and the neighboring buildings apart, killing all but three of the firemen instantly. Bodies and debris fell blocks away. One set of freight trucks from an NP boxcar at the freight house was blown eight blocks. Steel fishplates were stored in the freight house, and the explosion sent them spinning through the night cutting posts, people and buildings to shreds. The noise of the explosion brought hundreds more spectators to the site. Anything that could be utilized as an ambulance was pressed into service to begin the grisly task of removing the dead and wounded from the scene. Others fought the fire that was still raging through the wreckage. Suddenly, there was a third explosion which killed many of the rescuers and rained further debris on the wounded who were waiting to be evacuated.

Fearing yet another explosion, rescuers were reluctant to approach the scene too closely. They ultimately did, however, and the next morning the process of clean up began. Mass funerals were conducted for those who had been killed, but identification in some cases was difficult. All that was found of the fire chief was his helmet with some bloody residue inside.

As news of the event spread, collections were taken up for the relief of those who had suffered. The citizens of Missoula, recognizing there were few flowers in Butte (vegetation had long since disappeared because of the smelter fumes), harvested their gardens and sent over a ton of flowers to Butte on a special Northern Pacific train.

Afterward an investigation was held, and the warehouse owners were found guilty of leaving explosives in their warehouse at night. They were forced to flee the city lest they be subject to "vigilante justice."

Coxey's Army:

By the 1890's Montana ranked only behind Nevada in the production of silver. In May, 1893, plummeting gold reserves caused a drop in the stock market and a nation wide business panic. One of the remedies was the repeal of the Sherman Silver Purchase Act. Montana silver camps were devastated. Three thousand miners fled from Granite over night hoping to find employment elsewhere.

Many of Butte's silver mines closed as well. By December, 1893, 20,000 Montana workers were unemployed. The Northern Pacific and Union Pacific both went bankrupt as did the once mighty First National Bank of S.T. Hauser in Helena. Both Marcus Daly and William Clark brought to Butte gold coin which they lent to keep mines and businesses operating and some Butte workers employed. As a consequence, much of the anger felt in Butte turned outward toward the federal government rather than toward local business or state government.

In the summer of 1894 Jacob Coxey organized a silver protest march on Washington. Butte's "General William Hogan" and a crowd of unemployed miners commandeered a train in Butte's NP yard and started east to join the march. NP officials tried to stop the train, but sympathetic dispatchers and train men routed it through, accompanied by rousing celebrations at each station. In desperation Montana's governor was pressured to call out the National Guard which finally stopped the train at Forsyth, Montana, after a journey of over 400 miles.

As both the march and Hogan's abortive train ride were failing, influential mine owners called a convention at Helena in July, 1893, and formed a Montana Free Coinage Association. Marcus Daly was elected as its president. It too failed.

Silver would never again be a powerful force in the Montana economy. Copper was shown to be the commodity of the future for Butte. 1893 marked a transition point, and Coxey's Army was one of its most visible symbols. Hogan and his men would just be the first of a long line of miner's protests that would break out from time to time on the "Richest Hill on Earth."

MAIN LINE RIGHT-OF-WAY ALL SECURED

The right of way difficulties between the Montana Central Railway and the Northern Pacific and Montana and the Helena and Jefferson County Railroads have been adjusted by the Montana Central Railway paying $680.80 and deeding the necessary right of way.

Land has been sold the Montana Central Company at Clancy for terminal ground for $100.00.

The Land Department has reserved from sale right of way for the engine house track at Logan.

The Murray case for terminal properties at Butte is yet unsettled. It has been decided that the only claim that the Company has to the eighty acre tract near Butte is under the land grant, if not mineral land, as there was no adverse claim when the map of the road was filed.

A deed correcting a former conveyance for station grounds at Corvallis has been obtained. No additional cost.

NP Branch Line Reports   1896

Coxey's Army (actually Hogan's) atop its famous train in Butte Yard is depicted in this 1910 postcard commemorating the event. The train was able to travel to Forsyth before it was stopped by the National Guard. In the photo are an NP drovers' caboose, a billboard seded reefer, NP boxcar among other equipment.

The Summer "B" 1894 public timetable was issued before the 1896 reorganization which saw the NP not only restructure itself after its 1893 bankruptcy but absorb the variously named subsidiary branch lines into the parent system. It is interesting that the Butte Short Line is listed as the "Northern Pacific & Montana Branch." Other branches which had operated under the NP&M are listed separately. The BSL, Drummond & Philipsburg, Missoula & Bitteroot Valley, De Smet & Coeur d' Alene and others had originally been organized into the NP&M system. In 1894 passenger trains No. 1 & 2 are going through Helena rather than Butte. This would soon change. The Northern Pacific ran dining cars on its new transcontinental line from the very beginning, featuring five star cuisine. For $60 one could arrange for a nice excursion from St. Paul to Butte in a first class Pullman sleeper. The return could be arranged via the Great Northern through Great Falls.

FIRST-CLASS DINING CAR SERVICE. ALL MEALS 75C. EACH.

JE

3

NORTHERN PACIFIC & MONTANA BRANCH.

	No. 7 Butte Passenger. Daily.	Mls.	STATIONS.	No. 8 Bozeman Pass. Daily.	
....	5.58 a.m.	0	Lv....Bozeman......Ar.	1.00 p.m.	....
....	6 55 "	24	Lv........Logan........	11.59 a.m.	....
....	* 7.08 "	30	......Three Forks.....	11.50 "	....
....	7.23 "	43	......Sappington......	11.30 a.m.	....
Thur. only.	3.45AM / 4.30AM / 5.50AM	58 / 64 / 60	Ar....Harrison..Lv. / Ar.....Norris....Lv. / Ar......Pony.....Lv.	6.25AM / 4.40AM / 6.00AM	Thur. only.
....	8.00 a.m.	62	.......Whitehall......	10.54 a.m.	....
....	*8.16 "	69	......Pipestone......	*10.38 "	....
....	*9.04 "	85	......Homestake......	* 9.56 "	....
....	9.30 "	93	...M. U. Transfer....	9.30 "	....
....	9.40 a.m	95	Ar......Butte......Lv.	9.20 a.m.	....
....	12.10 p.m.	121	Ar.....Anaconda....Lv.	7.85 a.m.	....
....	11.20 a.m.	185	Ar....Deer Lodge....	7.27 a.m.	....
....	11.45 a.m.	146	Ar.....Garrison.....Lv.	7.05 a.m.	....

HELENA & JEFFERSON COUNTY, AND HELENA, BOULDER VALLEY & BUTTE BRANCH.

Mixed.	No. 10 Passenger. Daily.	Mls.	STATIONS.	No. 9 Passenger. Daily.	Mixed.
....	7.15 a.m.	.0	Lv......Helena......Ar.	6.30 p.m.	....
....	7.40 "	4.9	Lv..Prickly Pear Junc.Ar.	6.00 "	....
....	7.44 "	6.2	........Childs........	5.51 "	....
....	7.55 "	9.9	.....Montana City.....	5.39 "	....
....	8.10 "	14.6	.......Clancy........	5.22 "	....
....	8.14 "	15.9	.......Alhambra......	5.17 "	....
....	8.20 "	17.9	.......Hartwell......	5.10 "	....
....	8.30 a.m.	20.4	Ar......Jefferson....Lv.	5.00 p.m.	....
....	8.45 a.m.	22.2	........Corbin........	9.10 a.m.	....
....	8.55 a.m.	24.9	Ar......Wickes......Lv.	9.00 a.m.	....
....	10.28 a.m.	33.4	.......Amazon.......	3.57 p.m.	....
*10.50 a.m.	10.48 a.m.	37.4	.......Boulder......	3.37 p.m.	* 1.10 p.m.
11.20 "	....	45.0	.......Cataract......	....	12.40 "
11.45 "	....	48.6	......Red Rock......	....	12.15 "
11.55 a.m.	....	50.4	Ar......Calvin......Lv.	....	12 05 p.m.
....	10.50 a.m.	37.4	Lv......Boulder......Ar.	3.35 p.m.	....
....	11.05 a.m.	41.0	......Hot Springs.....	3.20 "	....
....	12.30 p.m.	58.0	Ar......Elkhorn......Lv.	2.00 p.m.	....

* Daily except Sunday between Boulder and Cataract. Saturday only between Cataract and Calvin.

MONTANA UNION RAILWAY.

Garrison Express. Daily.	Miles from G'r'sn	STATIONS.	Garrison Express. Daily.
....		Lv......Helena......Ar.	11.45 a.m.
7.05 a.m.	0	Lv......Garrison....Ar.	11.45 a.m.
7.27 "	10.9	Ar....Deer Lodge....	11.20 "
7.42 "	17.0	......Dempsey.......	11.07 "
7.47 "	26.1	......Race Track.....	11.03 "
8.17 a.m.	33.2	Ar.......Stuart.....Lv.	10.40 a.m.
8.50 a.m.	41.6	Ar......Anaconda....Lv.	9.00 a.m.
8.46 a.m.	44.4	Ar.....Silver Bow...Lv.	10.11 a.m.
9.05 a.m.	51.2	Ar.....Butte City...Lv.	9.55 a.m.

HELENA & RED MOUNTAIN BRANCH.

No. 101 Mixed. Mon. Wed. and Fri.	Mls.	STATIONS.	No. 102 Mixed. Mon. Wed. and Fri.
10.30 a.m.	.0	Lv......Helena......Ar.	2.30 p.m.
10.47 "	3.7	...Hotel Broadwater...	2.10 "
10.51 "	4.7	...Thermal Springs...	2.05 "
11.05 "	7.2	........Wades........	1.55 "
11.20 "	11.0	.......Gold Bar......	1.35 "
11.40 a.m.	14.1	......Moose Creek....	1.15 "
12.01 p.m	16.9	Ar......Rimini......Lv.	1.00 p.m.

HELENA & NORTHERN BRANCH.

No. 7 Accom. Daily Ex. Sun.	Mls.	STATIONS.	No. 8 Accom. Daily Ex. Sun.
3.30 p.m.	.0	Lv......Helena......Ar.	9.30 a.m.
4.00 "	9.1	....Clough Junction...	8.50 "
4.25 "	15.5	.........Cruse.......	8.30 "
5.00 p.m.	21.5	Ar.....Marysville...Lv.	8.05 a.m.

NOTE.—Where time is not shown opposite stations trains do not stop.

The Northern Pacific built the Butte Short Line in 1890 to accommodate heavy freight operations in and out of what had become Montana's premier mining center. The BSL was to rectify what many Butte residents felt was a mistake when the NP constructed its main line through Helena. With the acquisition of the Montana Union in 1896, the NP had a secondary main line to Butte, something not accomplished by any of the other roads until the Milwaukee built through 15 years later.

The truth is, however, the heavy freight traffic never materialized on the BSL. Rocky Fork coal, which had provided Kendrick with the impetus to scrap the HBV&B in favor of the BSL, was just too far from the city, and competing mines were able to provide coal cheaper and in greater quantity. While the mines lingered on into the 1930's, even the NP was forced to quit using the coal for its steam engines when it found it sparked, causing grass fires in eastern Montana. Mines at Chestnut near Bozeman, Coalstrip, and in Washington satisfied the railroad's needs. Evidence of Rocky Forks' lack of importance to the BSL can be found as early as 1896 in McHenry's Branch Line Report when he fails to mention coal when he lists commodities handled.

Additionally, the NP did not service any of the large mines or smelters in Butte directly. To reach its customers it needed to transfer commodities to other roads such as the Montana Union and the BA&P.

Where the BSL did play a role was in providing an alternative main line when the Mullan Tunnel route was unavailable or congested. At such times, as in 1949 when the tunnel caved in, traffic was rerouted over the BSL. Its light rail, short sidings, steep grades, and sharp corners, however, made operations over Homestake very difficult as trains became longer and heavier.

Passenger operations were where the BSL earned its way. From the earliest days the crack NP passenger trains such as the North Coast Limited traveled via Butte rather than Helena, providing generations of travelers with grand vistas and thrilling vantage points. Service on the BSL ended with the end of passenger service to Butte along the former NP. Operations did not long survive after the discontinuance of Amtrak's North Coast Hiawatha in 1979, almost 90 years after the Butte Short Line was constructed.

As long as the tracks remain, however, hope lingers that it will see service once again.

An east bound North Coast Limited departs Butte in a view depicted on this Northern Pacific postcard taken around 1950.

JM

The 1902 *Wonderland,* the Northern Pacific's tour book, refers to the Butte Short Line as the "Butte Air Line" in some of its photo captions. In an era before air travel, views such as the one above must have seemed a lot like flying. This view looks back at Butte from the rear vista dome on #26, the east bound North Coast Limited, above Skones in the late 1960's.

WRM

The Mullan Tunnel on the main line through Helena had caved in and trains were being diverted over the BSL when W.R. McGee took this photograph of train #602 with the 6006 set of four EMD FT's on the point at Homestake on March 11, 1949. The FT's were only five years old having been ordered in 1944. In 1950 the 6006 and its sisters would become the 5406 ABCD. The 6006A will be traded in to EMD in 1968. One of the section men sits on the steps of his company supplied box car house, placed at Homestake in 1908. The bulk of the 4,300 ton train is coming through Homestake Tunnel in the background.

This R.V. Nixon view looks east through the new summit cut which eliminated the Homestake Tunnel in 1956. Operations began in August, 1956, after an opening ceremony held near the east end of the new cut through the continental divide 300' south of the tunnel. In this photo the tracks have not yet been laid, and trains are still using tunnel #4, completed in 1890. Nixon is standing at what originally was known as Highview, the site of the notorious Precinct 34 scandal. Only a short spur track was left at Highview after the 1956 realignment. Material from this cut was used to start a new fill to eliminate tunnel #5, but the project was never completed.

JVM

By the 1950's the wooden lining of Homestake Tunnel needed to be replaced, and icicles threatened the new vista domes in winter. Rather than enlarge and reline the tunnel with concrete, a deep cut was excavated through the continental divide and the grade was moved 300' to the south. Trains started operating through the new cut on August 9, 1956. Tunnel #4 was filled with overburden, and the portals were collapsed.

There was also a plan to eliminate tunnel #5, Highview Tunnel. Dirt from the Homestake project went to build a new fill east of tunnel #5, but the project was never completed.

NP Will Bypass Historic Tunnel

New Track Planned in Butte Vicinity

BUTTE -- A contract for grading a new Northern Pacific railway line over the continental divide to bypass the historic Homestake Tunnel near Butte, has been awarded to the Albert Lalonde Co., Sidney, it was announced by H.R. Peterson, chief engineer.

Excavation is scheduled for completion by Sept. 30 and track laying, to be carried out by the railway's own forces, a month later. Total cost of the project is estimated at about $460,000.

When the 3,440-foot line change has been completed, the NP will abandon the 680-foot Homestake Tunnel. The new line, to be located about 300 feet south of the tunnel, will cross the divide at about the same elevation, 6,328 feet.

Homestake Tunnel was built in 1889 when the railway constructed its main line from Logan to Butte. The bore was drilled through solid rock. Regular train operations, which began May 26, 1890, gave Butte direct train service to the East [actually the last spike was driven March 29th, but train operations did not begin until June 14, 1890].

Billings Gazette   **April 8, 1955**

Old Homestake Tunnel Through Continental Divide Is No More

BUTTE (AP) -- The NP's Homestake Tunnel through the Continental Divide is no more. The 682-foot tunnel 11 miles southeast of Butte, now replaced by a half-million-dollar open cut, figured in a sensational attempted train robbery May 7, 1907, [this actually happened 5 miles east near Welch]....

Northern Pacific Railway's Logan-to-Butte Train 235 was the last to go through the tunnel Wednesday. The tunnel, completed in 1890, will be filled in and sealed.

The open cut is 3,475 feet long. It is 109 feet at its deepest, with a top width of 198 feet and bottom width of 60 feet.

First train through it was No. 25, the westbound North Coast Limited. Engineer Charles Graves, Livingston, one of the oldtimers on the Rocky Mountain Division, signaled the ceremony with a whistle blast.

Several residents of Butte, Livingston and Missoula were at the east end of the cut and watched the train break a green ribbon across the opening.

Division Supt. N.M. Lorentzen, Missoula, said the road also plans the elimination of shorter Highview Tunnel east of Homestake [not accomplished]. He said 797,000 tons of earth and rock -- some of ice age formation -- was removed to make the new cut, much of it by blasting.

"It will eliminate considerable cost of maintenance involved in operation of the old tunnel, and eliminate the hazard of falling rock," he said. "Formation of icicles in the tunnel also created a problem in the operation of the vista dome passenger cars.

Daily Missoulian   **August 10, 1956**

In July, 1996, Montana Rail Link #651 brings 20 loaded ballast cars down from the new quarry pit above Pipestone. The pit is around the ridge in the background, and Pipestone siding is one half mile to the east behind the camera. Both MRL and Burlington Northern load rock ballast here for company surfacing projects.

When Amtrak discontinued its North Coast Hiawatha in 1979, Burlington Northern's operations over the mountain district of the Butte Short Line became sporadic. Service to Alder via Whitehall and Twin Bridges (on the former Gaylord & Ruby Valley) continued because of a talc loading facility in Alder, but the mountain saw only an occasional local.

In May, 1980, severe floods washed out the Helena main line between Elliston and Garrison as well as the Boulder River bridge near Cardwell on the BSL. The bridge was quickly rebuilt in case the line was needed for diverted traffic, but few if any trains actually journeyed through Butte other than work trains.

In September, 1980, ARCO closed the Anaconda smelter and two years later the mines in Butte. As mining traffic dwindled, so did train operations over the BSL and were discontinued by late 1980. It was taken out of service between Whitehall and Butte.

In 1983 an Amtrak special movement traveled the hill when some inter-est was expressed in a rivial of service on the former North Coast Hiawatha route. The idea died for lack of funding.

Burlington Northern withdrew from Butte altogether on September 14, 1986, when it leased the former Montana Union line between Butte and Garrison to a new company named Montana Western, an affiliate of Raurus Railroad headquartered in Anaconda.

The following year, on October 31, 1987, Montana Rail Link was formed when Burlington Northern sold or leased most of the former Northern Pacific lines in Montana to the new company. The portion of the BSL from Logan to Whitehall and the branch from Whitehall to Alder were included in the sale. BN retained ownership of the mountain portion of the BSL as it still does in 1998. MRL continued operations to Alder, but these dwindled when the talc processing plant at Alder was relocated to Sappington.

In 1990 BN petitioned to abandon the Homestake Pass portion of the BSL. Washington Corporation (of which MRL is a subsidiary) moved to develop a ballast quarry above Pipestone siding, however, and in the negotiations which ensued, MRL obtained the trackage from Whitehall to mile post 52 above Spire Rock on October 13, 1992. BN withdrew its petition to abandon the remainder of the 18 miles between mile post 52 and Butte.

Currently the Pipestone quarry is being fully developed, and both MRL and BN ballast trains load crushed rock for resurfacing projects. The stone is of superior quality and reportedly holds up well to both wooden and cement tie usage. No trains operate above the quarry near mile post 47, and the line is closed at the Delmo Lake Road crossing.

Montana Western and Raurus Railroad operate over the former NP lines in Butte and as far east as mile post 68. While rumors abound concerning possible revivals to include possible tourist trains, as of this writing the tracks between mile post 52 and mile post 68 of the former BSL remain in place, owned by BN, but out of service.

Appendix

In 1893 the Northern Pacific went into bankruptcy. E.H. McHenry, surveyor of the Butte Short Line and later chief engineer of the NP, was appointed one of the receivers. He, J.W. Kendrick and other company officials were asked to evaluate the various properties and assess their worth. These pages are transcribed from the 1896 *BRANCH LINE REPORTS*: *Explanations Regarding the Accounts* by Edwin H. McHenry, Receiver, and J.W. Kendrick, General Manager. Only material relating to the lines discussed in this book has been included.

NORTHERN PACIFIC RAILROAD COMPANY.

St. Paul, Minn., March 2nd, 1896.

SUBJECT: NORTHERN PACIFIC & MONTANA RAILROAD:

Mr. EDWIN H. McHENRY,
Mr. FRANK G. BIGELOW,

Receivers, Northern Pacific Railroad Company,

St. Paul, Minn.

Gentlemen:--

Information concerning the Northern Pacific & Montana Railroad Lines:

CAPITALIZATION:

Bonded Debt $8,843,000.00
Rate of Interest 6%
Capital Stock 5,306,100.00

COST OF DUPLICATION:

		mls.	$ per m.	
	(Logan to Butte	70.877 mls.;	$25,000 per m.	$1,771,925.
1	(Sappington to Norris	20.895 "	14,000 " "	292,530.
	(Harrison to Pony	7.092 "	11,000 " "	78,012.
	(Jefferson to Boulder	16.955 "	26,000 " "	440,830.
	(Boulder to Basin	8.596 "	14,000 " "	120,344.
2	(Basin to Calvin	4.493 "	14,000 " "	62,902.
	(Boulder to Finn	9.000 "	13,000 " "	117,000.
	(Finn to Elkhorn	11.400 "	22,000 " "	250,800.
3	Clough Jct. to Marysville	12.576 "	22,000 " "	276,672.
4	Drummond to Rumsey	32.121 "	16,000 " "	513,936.
5	Missoula to Grantsdale	50.852 "	17,000 " "	864,484.
6	DeSmet to Idaho Boundary	109.517 "	21,000 " "	2,299,857.
		354.374		$7,089,292.

Construction Cost as per books $10,174,185.93

The foregoing lines will be reported upon in detail in six separate letters of this date.

Yours truly,

J.W. Kendrick,

General Manager.

NORTHERN PACIFIC RAILROAD COMPANY.

St. Paul, Minn., March 2nd, 1896.

SUBJECT: NORTHERN PACIFIC & MONTANA RAILROAD:

Mr. EDWIN H. McHENRY,
Mr. FRANK G. BIGELOW,

Receivers, Northern Pacific Railroad Company,

St. Paul, Minn.

Gentlemen:--

Information concerning the Northern Pacific & Montana Railroad Lines, LOGAN to BUTTE, SAPPINGTON to NORRIS, and HARRISON to PONY:

MILEAGE:

Logan to Butte	70.877 miles
Sappington to Norris	20.895 "
Harrison to Pony	7.092 "
Total	98.864 miles

DATE OF CONSTRUCTION, LOCATION AND BY WHOM OPERATED:

Until August, 1893, these lines were operated in connection with the Northern Pacific Railroad, in accordance with the provisions of a contract dated October 1, 1886, which contract covered a period of 999 years. Upon the appointment of Receivers for the Northern Pacific Railroad Company, the contract was cancelled, and in November, 1894, a new short term lease was made to the Receivers of the Northern Pacific Railroad Company.

The line from Logan to Butte connects with the Northern Pacific main line at Logan.

The line from Sappington to Norris is a spur of the Logan to Butte line.

The line from Harrison to Pony is a spur of the Sappington to Norris line.

PHYSICAL CONDITION &c.:

LOGAN TO BUTTE

The first section of this line is located up the valley of the Jefferson River, passing through the Jefferson River Cannon to Whitehall, the mountain terminal station at the foot of the east slope of the main range of the Rocky Mountains a distance of 38 miles.

The second section crosses the main range via Homestake Pass with a total rise of 2,100 feet from the river valley, or 6,328 feet above sea level, and descends 800 feet to the crossing of the Silver Bow Creek at Butte.

The grades of the first section do not exceed 26 feet to the mile, but the maximum grades are short and may be operated as virtual grades of 0.4% or less.

The second or Mountain Section has maximum grades of 2.2% which maximum rate is maintained almost continuously throughout the entire length of the section.

There are very valuable terminal grounds in the City of Butte and the road is unusually well provided with structures and all other necessary operating facilities, including good terminal buildings and facilities at both Logan and Butte.

The principal streams crossed are the Madison, Gallatin and Jefferson Rivers, requiring five Howe truss spans of 150 feet in length each.

The work on the mountain section is exceedingly heavy the cutting being in the rock. The trestles are large and frequent, containing about 9,000,000 feet B.M. of timber. About 40% of the bridging can be replaced by embankments by train-hauled material, and the remainder will have to be replaced by steel viaducts. The cost of this will be very heavy, but no estimate has been prepared covering it. It will not be necessary to do any work of this kind for some years, as the line is comparatively new, having been completed in 1890.

The track and roadbed are in first class condition. New 66-pound steel rail was laid on the main line throughout. The track is ballasted with gravel between Logan and Whitehall, and the mountain section is ballasted with material locally obtained, which is of a very good character. The track is fenced on both sides continuously, excepting the mountain and cannon section.

PHYSICAL CONDITION &c.:

SAPPINGTON TO NORRIS.

This line was completed in 1890. It is located upon the cannon of Antelope Creek, crossing the low divide at the head into one of the wide upland valleys of Willow Creek; thence it runs in a generally eastern direction to the present terminus at Norris, on the Madison River slope of the plateau. The maximum grades is the direction of traffic are 2.2%; averse to traffic 1.3%. The valley of Antelope Creek is exceedingly narrow and the cost of grading through that section was the heaviest. With the exception of the large trestle crossing the Norwegian Gulch, the remaining construction was comparatively light. The track was laid with new 56-pound steel rail and was surfaced from the sides, the natural material being very good. The general condition of the track is high.

PHYSICAL CONDITION &c.:

HARRISON TO PONY.

This line is located upon the valley of Willow Creek, to a point where it debouches from the mountain where the mining camp of Pony is located. The maximum grades in the direction of traffic are 3.2% with no grades adverse to traffic originating at Pony. The general condition of the track is good. The line was completed in 1890.

RIGHT-OF-WAY:

LOGAN TO BUTTE:

Seventeen and one-tenth (17.1) acres of right-of-way at an estimated cost of $375.00, remain to be purchased. An unsettled title, involving a portion of the right-of-way in Butte, may ultimately cost $5,000.00 additional.

SAPPINGTON TO NORRIS:

All right-of-way is secured.

HARRISON TO PONY:

There remain five and twenty-nine hundredths (5.29) acres of right-of-way to be secured, at an estimated cost of $212.00.

(CONNECTIONS WITH OTHER ROADS AND ABILITY TO DIVERT TRAFFIC: - Not included in this transcription.)

OPERATION:

LOGAN TO BUTTE:

Daily passenger trains run each way, connecting with the through main line passenger trains; also a daily freight train each way, with occasional extras when the business requires same.

SAPPINGTON TO NORRIS
and
HARRISON TO PONY.

The train service consists of a mixed train each way, weekly, work being performed by the regular way freight train from Butte.

CHARACTER OF TRAFFIC AND VALUE OF ROAD AS A FEEDER:

LOGAN TO BUTTE,
SAPPINGTON TO NORRIS,
HARRISON TO PONY.

These lines should be considered together, as the latter two are merely spurs of the former. Traffic originating on these lines consists almost entirely of ores, limestone and lime, stock and hay, and the traffic carried to these lines consists of miners' supplies, lumber and miscellaneous articles of almost every description used in the city of Butte and that vicinity. The eastern portion of the line lies in a well settled valley, devoted principally to agriculture and stock raising from which a considerable traffic is derived.

The main line revenue from interchange traffic was, for the year ending June 30, 1895, $458,334.20. A share of this traffic could, however, be secured by the Northern Pacific through the Montana Union road (owned jointly by the Northern Pacific and Union Pacific.) It could be, perhaps, fair to estimate the value of these lines as a feeder as 40% of two-thirds of the sum above referred to, 40% being the estimated profit over Operating Expenses and Taxes, and two-thirds being the proportion of the total interchange traffic which would be lost if the control of the lines should be lost by the Northern Pacific.

40% of 2/3 of $458,334.20 . . . . $122,222.45

To which should be added the Net
    Earnings of the lines in question 54,559.24

            Total $176,781.69

There has recently been constructed a spur 5.6 miles long from Whitehall to a point at which the Parrott Silver & Copper Company has located a smelter. This spur cost about $60,000, the entire amount of which was advanced by the Parrott Company under an agreement that the Northern Pacific & Montana will reimburse the Parrott Company by a refund of one-half of the earnings of the Northern Pacific and Montana from business to and from the smelter. When the Parrott Company shall have been entirely reimbursed, the spur is to become the property of the Northern Pacific & Montana. In the meantime, it may be expected that the business of this smelter will largely increase the earnings of the Northern Pacific & Montana Railroad locally, and also those of the Northern Pacific main line, but it should be remembered that for a time a portion of this increase in gross earnings must be applied to pay the cost of the spur.

It should be remembered that the so-called Net Earnings of the branches mentioned in this letter, are the results of accounts kept upon what may be called, for brevity, the "double mileage" basis, subject to various exceptions, however, full particulars of which may be found by examination of lease of November 12, 1894, under which the Northern Pacific Receivers are now operating all the lines of the Northern Pacific & Montana road. Had the branches been allowed a greater proportion of interchange earnings, the net result of the branch operations would have been better, but the profit to the main line out of its proportion of the earnings, would have been less. It should be noted too that 40% of the main line gross earnings from interchange business has been treated as a profit over operating expenses and taxes. This percentage is an arbitrary estimate.

FUTURE PROSPECTS:

LOGAN TO BUTTE,
SAPPINGTON TO NORRIS,
HARRISON TO PONY.

There is every reason to suppose that the business of these lines will gradually increase. The business which is expected from the smelter recently built by the Parrott Company, near Whitehall, is however, the only item of increase of which we have any definite knowledge at this time. Butte is a prosperous mining centre and no one expects anything except a continuation of its property.

Yours truly,

J.W. KENDRICK

General Manager.

NORTHERN PACIFIC RAILROAD COMPANY

St. Paul, Minn., March 4th, 1896.

SUBJECT: NORTHERN PACIFIC & MONTANA RAILROAD

EDWARD D. ADAMS, ESQ.,

Chairman, Mills Building, New York.

Dear Sir:--

Transmitting report of General Manager concerning the Northern Pacific & Montana Railroad lines. While these lines are all included under one charter, in the majority of cases the lines are not connected and must be considered independently.

LOGAN TO BUTTE:

The most valuable line is that between Logan and Butte, the ownership of which is almost a vital necessity to the Northern Pacific Railroad. There is no reason to doubt that the traffic secured by this line will continue to increase for many years. The location of the great works of the Parrot Copper & Silver Mining Company, near Whitehall, is an event of very great importance, and the increased business created is expected to be very large. The grades in the valley sections are very low, and all the rise and fall is concentrated in a single summit. The mileage between the two junction points on the main line at Logan and Garrison, is 3 1/2 miles less than the main line, and it is quite possible that at some time in the future of Company will conduct the greater part of its through freight business via this route. The present obstacle to such operation is the partial ownership of the Northern Pacific R.R. in the Montana Union Railway; equal shares of this stock are owned by the Northern Pacific R.R. Co. and the Union Pacific Railway. A special report covering the Montana Union Railway will be forwarded to you later. The construction of the line to Norris and Pony appears to have been unfortunate, as the anticipated business was not secured, the mines closing down soon after the construction of the branch line. This was due to the prevalent and universal mining depression which has prevailed during the past few years on account of the low prices of silver and lead. There is very good reason to anticipate a general revival, however, in which these lines will share. Twenty-two miles of new line could be constructed to a very good advantage by extending the Parrot Smelter Branch southwardly up the Valley of the Jefferson River to Twin Bridges, which is located at the confluence of the Ruby, Beaver Head and Big Hole Rivers, which unite to form the Jefferson. There is a resident population of about 5,000 people which would be tributary to the line at that point. These people are engaged in mining, agriculture, horse and cattle raising. The great part of the trade of this region is now tributary to the Utah & Northern Branch of the Union Pacific at Dillon. The construction is exceedingly light, and the line will not cost to exceed $12,000.00 per mile. It may also become advisable to connect with the H.B.V. & B. and Elkhorn Branch of the N.P. & M., by making a connection with the Elkhorn branch at the station of Finn, which would involve the construction of a line of 21 miles in length following the course of the Boulder River, connecting with the Butte Line at the station of Jefferson Island. No great amount of new business would be secured, however, the only object in such construction being to avoid expensive operation, maintenance and renewal of the mountain section between Jefferson and Boulder, as will appear later. This connection if built would cost about $11,000 per mile or $231,000.00.

JEFFERSON TO CALVIN:

The line from Jefferson to Calvin was constructed in 1886-1887 at the instance of ex-Governor S.T. Hauser, and associates, who also obtained the construction contract at excessive prices. It was constructed to gain access to some mines in the vicinity of Calvin, which were supposed at the time to be very rich, and it was ultimately expected to extend the line to Butte, complete location surveys and estimates having been prepared with this end in view. Through the efforts of the former Chief Engineer, J.W. Kendrick, this project was abandoned in favor of the existing line between Logan and Butte. It would have been a great misfortune had the original intentions been carried out, as the mountain summit is very high, and the projected grades were 3.2%. The line would have had less tributary local business, and would not have served its purpose nearly so well in other respects. The expectations regarding the mines at Calvin proved unfounded, and the mines have furnished no business to the road. Subsequently some mines of considerable promise have been developed near Basin, and some valuable business may be secured at that point. Within two years after the construction of the line it was paralleled throughout its entire distance, by the main line of the Montana Central Branch of the Great Northern. This line is much better in its construction and grades, and the service in infinitely superior. In consequence of this later construction of the line it is improbable that we can ever compete with the Montana Central Railway upon equal terms, as the volume of the local business does not justify a better service than that which is now furnished.

The Elkhorn branch was also constructed at the instance of Mr. Hauser and others, who asserted that a daily ore business amounting to 400 tons would be afforded by the mines at Elkhorn and vicinity. It is hardly necessary to state the tonnage never averaged, at any time, one-tenth the amount promised, and it now appears that the ore supplies in the principal mine "The Elkhorn" are nearly exhausted. There are other mines in the vicinity which have been worked spasmodically, and which may yet develop, but the probabilities of any considerable tonnage from this source are exceedingly intangible. The terms of the contract under which this branch was constructed was exceedingly favorable, presenting a great contrast to the prices awarded on the previous section between Jefferson and Calvin, as a comparison of the following items will show:--

	Jefferson to Calvin	Boulder to Elkhorn
Solid rock, per cubic yard	1.90	.90
Loose rock, per cubic yard	.85	.40
Earth, per cubic yard	.30	.16
Timber in structures, per M.	42.00	20.00

It will soon be necessary to renew the heavy mountain trestles between Jefferson and Boulder, at an estimated cost of $80,000. In addition the constant use of sand on the sharp curvature and steep grades causes a very rapid rail wear. The cost of operation is very high, both on account of physical condition, and the thin volume of traffic. It is possible that a careful estimate will demonstrate the advisability of abandoning the mountain section between Jefferson and Boulder, and the unproductive section between Basin and Calvin, and that a sufficient reduction in cost of operation and maintenance would be secured to justify the construction of the connection with the Butte Line, previously mentioned, between Finn and Jefferson Island. As the steel recovered from these would be sufficient to complete the connection, the net additional cost of the latter line would probably not exceed $8,000 per mile. I would not care to make a recommendation to this effect, however, until I have had an opportunity for a more careful analysis of the subject. To sum up I consider the existing lines of exceedingly small value to the Company, and consider their construction as a very unfortunate mistake.

(HELENA & NORTHERN, DRUMMOND AND PHILLIPSBURG, MISSOULA & BITTER ROOT VALLEY, DE SMET TO IDAHO BOUNDARY - Not included in this transcription.)

As the estimates accompanying the report show the cost of duplicating the entire Northern Pacific & Montana system to-day would be but $7,080,292, which is considerably less than the construction cost, as shown by the Auditor's books, or the bonded debt. I am loath to make a recommendation as to the rental which the Northern Pacific R.R. Co. should be expected to pay, as so many elements enter into a question of this kind. While it appears that the value of the business furnished to the main line is sufficient to pay the interest on the present bonded indebtedness, it is obviously beyond the power of the main line to pay rentals on this basis, without creating a heavy deficit in the amounts available for its own fixed charges. I believe a rental of 4% upon the estimated cost of duplication is the utmost that could be expected, as many of these branches have no power to divert traffic, and in some instances at least the investment is unproductive and valueless.

Yours very truly,

E. H. McHENRY,

Receiver.

NORTHERN PACIFIC RAILROAD COMPANY.

St. Paul Minn., March 6th, 1896.

SUBJECT: ROCKY FORK & COOKE CITY RAILROAD.

EDWARD D. ADAMS, ESQ.,

Chairman, Mills Building, New York.

Dear Sir:

Transmitting herewith report of General Manager J.W. Kendrick, concerning the Rocky Fork & Cooke City Railroad.

It is not possible to thoroughly cover this subject except in connection with the Rocky Fork Coal Company, a report upon which I will send you later. As you will note in the body of the report, the road was a very easy one to construct, and is without any physical features of importance, or engineering difficulties of any nature, excepting the Yellowstone Bridge, near the junction. Even after allowing for an extraordinary discount on bonds, the reported cost was far in excess of the necessary and proper expenditure. The road was constructed solely for the purpose of hauling coal, and as shown, the rates obtained are so low as to leave no profit to the main line from the business. We have repeatedly figured on the cost of hauling coal and our results indicate that a rate of 0.6 per ton mile represents the cost of hauling coal under ordinary conditions over 1% grades, including the empty return of cars over the whole distance. This empty car mileage is an invariable accompaniment of this class of business. In the present case the commercial coal delivered to either Butte or Helena must be hauled across two summits, and the probabilities are that the cost is higher rather than under the amount estimated. I think it can be demonstrated that the Company can purchase coal to much better advantage elsewhere, and accordingly almost the whole cost of operating this line may be considered a dead loss.

Yours truly,

E.H. McHenry

Receiver.

St. Paul, Minn., April 5th, 1896.

Geo. R. Sheldon, Esq.,

Chairman Bondholders Committee N.P.& M.R.R.CO.,

4 Wall Street, New York, N.Y.

Dear Sir:--

I returned yesterday from an inspection of the Northern Pacific & Montana Railroad Company and beg to submit the following informal report of the inspection of the property and its future prospects.

The Northern Pacific have not yet furnished me with certain statements as to earnings and expenses which I have requested but I expect to have them in a few days and will at an early date forward you formal report.

As you are no doubt aware the property consists of nine branch lines which go to make up the system of 363 miles.

As the conditions pertaining to the earnings, division of earnings, and expenses of these branches, varies for each branch, each must be treated separately:

SAPPINGTON - NORRIS BRANCH:

The Sappington - Norris Branch is 20.6 miles long. The line runs through a comparatively easy country and its construction is not expensive; certainly very much less than $25,000. a mile. The track is in poor condition and there is little evidence of any work having been done in its maintenance since its construction.

HARRISON - PONY BRANCH:

The Harrison - Pony Branch 6.3 miles long is little more than a spur from the Sappington Branch. The cost per mile probably did not exceed $7000. The condition of track is very poor and little or no work has been expended in maintenance since its construction. The buildings on both branches are extravagant as are also the side-track facilities. At the termini of these branches, Norris and Pony respectively are deposits of low grade silver ore. Few of the mines have been developed to any extent. A small number of cars of ore are being shipped at this time but certainly not enough to warrant the building of a railroad to distribute their output, and it is difficult to understand from a railroad point of view why these branches were ever constructed. The train service at present consists of one train a week.

LOGAN - BUTTE BRANCH:

The first forty miles of this branch runs through a comparatively easy country, the average cost of construction probably being in the neighborhood of from $14,600. to $16,000. per mile; the balance 25.5 miles is heavy work and a large number of rock cuts and high trestles and no doubt cost fully $25,000. per mile. The grades in this latter section are heavy, resulting in expensive operation. The track is in fair condition and has been fairly well maintained since construction. There is some little farming land tributary to the line between Whitehall and Logan, the distance between these stations being 38 miles. At the former station some little business originates from the mines south of this station. From Whitehall to Butte the country is unproductive and no business originates from it now nor is it likely there ever will, excepting small shipments of wood to Butte. The terminals at Butte are ample and in good shape.

The Northern Pacific & Montana reaches none of the smelters or concentrators directly but through some one of the other lines, viz. Montana Central, Montana Union, Butte, Anaconda & Pacific. On all other such shipments & switching charge accrues which although in most cases is paid by the consignor works to some disadvantage in competitive business. This practically also leaves only those industries located off Montana Central Railroad tracks open for competitive business between Union Pacific and Northern Pacific & Montana, and Montana Central diverts all business to the Great Northern. The Northern Pacific and Montana control a fair proportion of shipments of merchandise, etc., from the East. The different shipments from Butte consist principally of copper, pig and matte, principally the former, which is hauled to Logan and delivered to the main line of the Northern Pacific, and from which the latter get the through haul East.

One of the largest smelters at Butte is now being moved to Whitehall which will increase the earnings of the line considerably as the ores will be hauled from Butte to Whitehall and smelted at that point; the product of the smelter going from Whitehall East over the Northern Pacific. The coal for the smelter will be hauled from points on the Northern Pacific. Such a location will secure all of the business of the smelter to the branch line as well as increase the business of the main line. The branch is essentially a feeder of the Northern Pacific, both in its freight and passenger business and is of value to it. It is of value to the Great Northern.

JEFFERSON - CALVIN BRANCH:

The Jefferson - Calvin line is 29.8 miles long. This branch does not connect directly with the main line of the Northern Pacific but through the Helena & Jefferson County Railroad, 13.4 miles long, from Prickly Pear Junction, Northern Pacific main line to Jefferson. Some ten miles of this line is heavy work but the balance is medium and the average cost of construction probably did not exceed $12,000 to $15,000 per mile. The country through which the line runs is poor and is not a producer. A small amount of business originates from Basin, four miles from Calvin. There are a few mines in this vicinity which are now being worked to a small extent, the ore being concentrated at that point, the concentrates being shipped to East Helena. At Calvin no business at all originates except at this time small shipments of wood which go to Elkhorn on the Boulder-Elkhorn Branch.

The conditions of the line from Jefferson to Boulder 16.8 miles is in only fair condition and little work has been expended in its maintenance. From Boulder to Calvin the line is in very poor condition, the ties being rotten and the property greatly depreciated. The Montana Central Railroad runs through Basin and controls nearly all of what little business there is on account of better service, other than concentrates. There is tri-weekly train service on this branch.

BOULDER - ELKHORN BRANCH:

The Boulder - Elkhorn Branch is 20.4 miles long. The first nine miles of the line is easy work, probably not costing more than $10,000 per mile. From there to Elkhorn the work is heavy, the average cost being about from $16,000 to 18,000 per mile. No work has been expended the maintenance of this proportion of track, and on account of sliding cuts, twenty degree curve and four percent grade it is a difficult piece of property to maintain and operate economically. At Elkhorn there is located a mine and mill whose product is bullion which goes by express and means no earnings to the Railroad except what little supplies are hauled into the town of five hundred inhabitants and the wood required for the mill. It is claimed that the mine is about worked out and although there are a number of small mines in the vicinity, the ore is of low grade and cannot at this time be profitably worked. If the Elkhorn mine is closed there will be absolutely no business originating from or going to Elkhorn and the property from Boulder to Elkhorn will practically be valueless.

(CLOUGH JUNCTION TO MARYSVILLE, DRUMMOND - RUMSEY BRANCH, MISSOULA - GRANTSDALE BRANCH, - Not included in this transcription.)

The above is only a general resume of my inspection, and the investigation of the accounts of the Northern Pacific and Montana may to some extent change the figures above given.

After having had access to the accounts I will be able to give you more definite figures as to what these branches are worth and their value to the Northern Pacific Railroad as feeders. I cannot at this time see that they are of any value to any other Railroad Company.

Very truly yours,

L.S. Miller.

NORTHERN PACIFIC RAILROAD COMPANY.

St. Paul Minn., March 2, 1896.

SUBJECT: ROCKY FORK & COOKE CITY RAILROAD.

Mr. EDWIN H. McHENRY
Mr. FRANK G. BIGELOW,

Receivers, Northern Pacific Railroad Company,

St. Paul, Minnesota

Gentlemen:

Information concerning the Rocky Fork & Cooke City Railroad:

CAPITALIZATION:

Bonded Debt . . . . None.
Capital Stock $2,000,000.00

MILEAGE:

Laurel, Montana, to Red Lodge, Montana . . . . 44.373 miles
Track to Mines at Red Lodge . . . . 1.058 "

Total . . . . 45.431 miles

DATE OF CONSTRUCTION, LOCATION AND BY WHOM OPERATED:

This road was completed in 1890, and until August 15, 1893, was operated by the Northern Pacific Railroad Company, the owner of its entire capital stock. Since August 15, 1883, the road has been operated by the Receivers of the Northern Pacific Railroad Company, as owners of the capital stock of the Rocky Fork & Cooke City Railroad Company. There is and has been, so far as I can learn, no traffic contract, lease or agreement of any kind covering the operation of this line by the Northern Pacific Railroad or its Receivers.

The line connects with the Northern Pacific main line at Laurel, Montana.

PHYSICAL CONDITION &c.:

The road is located up the Clark's Fork of the Yellowstone diverging and following upward, the valley of a lateral tributary call the Rocky Fork. With the exception of a Howe truss bridge of three spans, 157 feet each, the construction is of the lightest possible description. The valley floor is very even and but little bridging is required by the stream. The track was laid with new 56-pound steel rail, and the ballast is of satisfactory character. The track is maintained in good condition. The Howe truss bridge referred to, crossed the Yellowstone River, cost $25,000.00, and at some time in the future will require replacement by a permanent steel superstructure and concrete piers, at a cost of about $50,000.00.

RIGHT OF WAY:

All secured.

(CONNECTIONS WITH OTHER ROADS AND ABILITY TO DIVERT TRAFFIC - Not included in this transcription.)

ADVISABILITY OF BUILDING THIS LINE IF IT WERE NOT ALREADY IN EXISTENCE:

If the Red Lodge coal, which is mined at the southern terminus of this road, could be obtained at a reasonable price, it would probably be worth while to build a line to Red Lodge for the purpose of securing coal for the use of locomotives on the Northern Pacific Railroad, between the Missouri River and Missoula. Under the terms of the existing contract between the Northern Pacific and the Rocky Fork Coal Company, which contract has been adopted by the former Receivers, Messrs. Oakes, Payne and Rouse, the Northern Pacific is obliged to take a large amount of coal from Red Lodge and therefore needs the Rocky Fork & Cooke City Railroad. Unless the contract with the Coal Company can be very materially modified, I shall consider it necessary to continue to recommend the construction of the Rocky Fork & Cooke City Railroad if it were not already there.

COST OF DUPLICATION:

Estimated at not more than $16,000.00 per mile; 45.431 miles: $590,603.00.

OPERATION:

The volume of business on this line varies with the output of the mines. In the spring and early summer, the traffic amount to about 30 cars of coal per day, which is handled by a mixed train which runs each way daily, except Sunday. In the fall and winter months, the additional coal to be moved makes it necessary to run an extra freight train about three times each week. The grades are such that the number of loaded cars hauled toward the main line is only limited by the number of empty cars which the engine is able to haul to the mines from the main line.

(CHARACTER OF TRAFFIC AND VALUE OF ROAD AS A FEEDER: - Not included in this transcription.)

FUTURE PROSPECTS:

It is not likely there will be any increase in the business of the Rocky Fork & Cooke City Railroad in the near future, except as the country becomes more thickly populated, there will be an increase in the consumption of coal, in which increase the Red Lodge mines will undoubtedly share. There are quite a number of coal mines in Montana which are situated much nearer to Helena, Butte and Anaconda, and the Red Lodge mines now labor, and will continue to do so, under great disadvantage on that account.

Yours truly,

J.W. KENDRICK

General Manager.

Sources Consulted

Across the Continent Via the Northern Pacific: From the Lakes & Mississippi River to the Pacific, Columbia River, Puget Sound & Alaska. St. Paul: A.C. Riley, [c.1890].

Along the Scenic Highway: Through the Land of Fortune. N.p.: Northern Pacific Railway, [c.1915].

Anaconda Standard [Anaconda, MT]. 1888-1906.

Athern, Robert. G. *Union Pacific Country.* Chicago: Rand, McNally, 1971.

Bates, Grace. *Gallatin County: Places & Things Present & Past.* N.p.: n.p., 1994.

Billings Gazette [Billings, MT]. 1888-9, 1955.

Bozeman Chronicle [Bozeman, MT]. 1891.

Burlingame, Merrill G. *Gallatin County's Heritage: A Report of Progress 1805-1976.* N.p.: n.p., [c.1976].

Butte Daily Intermountain [Butte, MT]. 1891.

Butte Daily Miner [Butte, MT]. 1887-1920.

Cheney, Roberta Carkeek. *Names on the Face of Montana.* Missoula: Mountain, 1983.

Clark, R. Milton. "Railroad Map of Montana." Montana: Unpublished map, 1996.

Cohen, Stan. Private collection. Missoula, MT.

Daily Independent: Helena [Helena, MT]. 1888-1920.

Daily Missoulian [Missoula, MT]. 1895-1956

Engineering and Mining Journal. 1890.

Ferrel, Mallory Hope. "Utah & Northern: the Narrow Gauge that Opened a Frontier." *Colorado Rail Annual No. 15* . Golden: Colorado Railroad Museum, 1981.

Glasscock, C.B. *War of the Copper Kings.* New York: Grosset & Dunlap, 1935.

Hamilton, James McClellan. *History of Montana: From Wilderness to Statehood.* Portland: Binfords & Mort, 1970.

Haynes, F. J. Collected photographs. Montana Historical Society, Helena.

Hersey, A.H. "Mines and Towns of Jefferson County, Montana." *The Northwest Magazine* August, 1985: 23-5.

Jefferson Valley Museum, Inc. Archives. Whitehall, MT.

Jefferson Valley Zephyr [Whitehall, MT]. 1894-1898.

Johnson, Dale L. "Andrew B. Hammond: Education of a Capitalist on the Montana Frontier." Diss. U of Montana, 1976.

Journal [Butte, MT]. 1902.

Lahr, John. Private collection. Butte, MT.

Lewty, Peter J. *To the Columbia Gateway: The Oregon Railway and the Northern Pacific, 1879-1884.* Pullman: Washington State UP, 1987.

Livingston Enterprise [Livingston, MT]. 1914.

Malone, Michael P. *The Battle for Butte: Mining and Politics on the Northern Frontier, 1864-1906.* U of Washington P, *1981.*

Marsh, George D., Ed. *Copper Camp.* Workers of the Writers' Program in the State of Montana. New York: Hastings House, 1943.

McGee, Warren R. Private collection. Livingston, MT.

Minister, P. F. "Quarrying of Limestone at Lime Spur, Montana." *Society for Industrial Archaeology, Klepetko Chapter Newsletter* Spring, 1997: 5-7.

Missoula Gazette [Missoula, MT]. 1889-1890.

Montana. American Historical Society. Chicago: n.p., 1921.

Myers, Rex. "The Butte Rail Connection: Mining and Transportation, 1880-1980." *The Speculator: A Journal of Butte and Southwest Montana History* Summer, 1984: 30-36.

Not In Precious Metals Alone: A Manuscript History of Montana. Bozeman: Montana State Historical Society, 1976.

Montana Weekly Record [Helena, MT]. 1901-03.

Nolan, Edward W. *Northern Pacific Views: Railroad Photography of F. J. Haynes, 1876-1905.* Helena: Montana Historical, 1983.

Northern Pacific Papers. University of Montana Archives, Missoula.

Peterson, Allen. Private Collection. Whitehall, MT.

Railway World. 1889-1890.

Renz, Louis Tuck. *The History of the Northern Pacific Railroad.* Fairfield: Ye Galleon, 1980.

Rocky Mountain Husbandman [White Sulpher Springs, MT]. 1895.

Ross, Norma DesJardin. "A Family Story of Morrison Cave." *Society for Industrial Archaeology, Klepetko Chapter Newsletter* Spring, 1997: 7-9.

Rowe, Jesse Perry. *Some Economic Geology of Montana. Bulletin No. 50, Geological Series No.3.* Missoula: U of Montana P, 1908.

Schrenk, Lawrence. "The Montana Union Railway." Ms., [1995?].

Smalley, Eugene V. "Butte, Montana: The Greatest Mining City of the World . . .Its Wealth and Progress . . .Its Mines, Mills and Smelters." *The Northwest Magazine* (December, 1890): 17-33.

-----, *History of the Northern Pacific Railroad.* Mid American Frontier. New York: G.P. Putam's Sons, 1883. Arno: New York, 1975.

Taber, Thomas T. *The Histories of the Independently Operated Railroads of Montana.* Unpublished manuscript, 1960. Montana Historical Society.

Three Forks Herald [Three Forks, MT]. 1909-1910.

United States. Census Bureau. Federal Census. 1900 and 1910.

-----. Dept. of Interior. Geological Survey. *Butte, Montana--Special Folio, 1897.*

-----. Dept. of Interior. Geological Survey. *Guidebook of the Western United States: Part A. The Northern Pacific Route.* Washington: U.S., 1915.

-----. Interstate Commerce Commission. Valuation: Northern Pacific Railway Company. Date of inventory, 1917. 1929.

Venable, William J. Private collection. Livingston, MT.

Whitehall Centennial 1890-1990. [c.1990].

Winser, Henry J. *The Great Northwest: A Guide Book and Itinerary For the Use of Tourists and Travellers Over the Lines of the Northern Pacific Railroad, the Oregon Railway and Navigation Company and the Oregon and California Railroad.* New York: Putnam's Sons, 1883.

-----. *The Great Northwest: A Guide Book and Itinerary For the Use of Tourists and Travellers Over the Lines of the Northern Pacific Railroad, the Oregon Railway and Navigation Company and the Oregon and California Railroad.* St. Paul: Riley Brothers, 1886.

Zupan, Shirley, and Harry J. Owens. *Red Lodge: Saga of a Western Area.* Billings: Frontier, 1979.

WRM

W.R. McGee captions this September 8, 1948, photo, "Butte extra - 1733 west with 50 cars mostly cattle which equals 1799 tons. A rare treat for trainmen to go to Butte in daytime. We were to make a Butte UP connection. We needed two helpers. Locomotive #4019, a 2-8-8-2 just bumped from road service in the Cascades by new F7 diesels, and #1761, a 2-8-2, an old standby on the NP's Rocky Mountain Division. This was a good day for pictures in this roadless area, so I walked over the moving cars to make some. This is Bridge #52 west of Spire Rock.

Index

Hawkins, Charles 7
Haynes, F.J. 15, 21-22 33, 41, 75, 80
Helena 7-19, 22, 26, 28-29, 36-37, 42, 88, 91, 93-4, 106
Helena & Jefferson County 12, 91, 104
Helena & Northern 102
Helena & Southern 49
Helena, Boulder Valley & Butte 10, 12, 14-15, 17, 21, 44, 93, 101
Hell Gate River 87
Henderson, sheriff 59, 67
Hennessey, D.J. 28
Heyman, Abe 23
Highview 21, 31-32, 72-3, 75, 78, 80-1, 95
Highview Siding 33
Highview Tunnel 34, 80, 95
Hill, James J. 9-10, 12, 16
Hogan, Gen. William 91
Homestake 10, 19, 22, 24-6, 29-30, 32-3, 46, 48, 52, 57, 59, 63, 68-9, 72-3, 83-4, 93-4
Homestake Ballast Pit 69-70, 73
Homestake Creek 31, 68
Homestake Lake 70, 72
Homestake Pass 14-15, 18, 21, 29, 31, 33, 44, 50, 53, 55, 81, 96, 98
Homestake Siding 33, 70, 74,
Homestake Tunnel 19, 21, 23, 64, 70, 73-5 80, 94-5
Hoppers Tunnel 67
Hortrum, G.C. 83
Howard, conductor 49
Howe, George 29
Hubbard 42
Hunter, photographer 41
Hutchinson building, Logan 37

Ingleside Spur 30, 32
Interstate Commerce Commission 12, 52, 55, 58
Irvine, George W. 23

Jack, election canvasser 79
Jacobs, Albert 47
Jefferson Bar 19, 26-27, 31, 42
Jefferson Canyon 14-17, 19, 31, 40, 42, 44, 98
Jefferson City 12, 97, 101-2, 104
Jefferson County 62
Jefferson Island 25, 29, 31-32, 44, 101-2
Jefferson Island Siding 26
Jefferson River 13, 15, 17, 30-31, 36, 38-9, 41,43, 49, 98
Jefferson Valley 12-13, 16, 31-32, 49, 101
Jocko Valley 8
Jones, brakemen 29
Jullien, Col. Phil 23

Keefe & Gallagher 79
Keefe & Green 15, 17, 19-22, 27, 40, 72, 78-9
Keefe , Michael H. 15, 17-20, 22, 27, 73, 78-9
Keith, engineer 8
Kendrick, J.W. 14, 16, 25, 27-8, 44, 93, 97, 100-1, 103, 106
Kenyon, Connell Commercial Co. 90
Kessler, Capt. 20
Kinney, E.C. 17
Kone, Max 67

Lake Pend d'Oreille 87
Lanser, illustrator 36
Larson, A.W. 19
Laurel 14, 105
Legget, John 13
Lewis & Clark Caverns National Monument 31, 42
Lewis & Clark Expedition 38
Lewis, Alderman 23, 68
Lewis, Capt. Meriweather 38, 39
Lewis Spur 26, 32-3, 68
Lime Spur 30-2, 42-3
Little Blackfoot 7
Livingston 10, 32, 37-8, 67, 75, 89, 95
Lloyd, sheriff 20
Locomotive #31 46
Locomotive #83 23
Locomotive #102 33, 63-4
Locomotive #131 46
Locomotive #161 46
Locomotive #285 7
Locomotive #350 11
Locomotive #583 44
Locomotive #598 48
Locomotive #721 47
Locomotive #982 90
Locomotive #1213 74
Locomotive #1750 60
Locomotive #2120 60, 67
Locomotive #3100 46
Locomotive "The Logan" 7
Locomotives #5406 ABCD 94
Locomotives #6006 ABCD 94
Logan 10, 15, 20, 22-3, 25-33, 36-8, 40-2, 51,91, 93, 95-8, 100-1, 104
Logan, John V. 82
Lombard 10
Lord, Henry W. 89
Lorentzen, N.M. 95
Lourey, Daniel M. 89
Lovell, WY 43
Lumber Spur 33
Lyons, Capt. 23

Madison County 41
Madison River 17, 30, 36, 38, 98-9
Madison Valley 31
Maezcher's store, Logan 37
Maginnis, Martin 79
Mainstreeter 93
Mansfield, W.R. 29
Marney, Clifford 47
Martin, Aleck 23
Marysville 97, 105
Matthews Bros. & Carrick 19, 21, 23, 55
Maude S Creek 84
McArthur, Angus 83
McCaig, James 9, 14, 19, 23, 28-9
McCarrey, Mr. 82
McCullagh, William 83
McEvoy, John 79
McGee, Warren 56, 61, 94
McGonigle, engineer 44
McHenry, Edwin H. 14, 16, 19, 22-6, 27-9, 40, 73, 93, 97-8, 102-3, 105
McTague, Mr. 83
Meaderville 13, 29, 79
Melrose 17
Metropolitan Electric Railway 35
Mikesell, C. 46
Miller, L.S. 105

Mills, Mr. 25
Milwaukee Road 8, 16, 30-1, 37-40, 44, 47, 73, 86, 88, 93
Missoula 8, 10, 16, 78, 95, 97, 105-6
Missoula County 19
Missoula River 87
Missoula & Bitter Root Valley 18, 92, 102
Missouri River 7, 16-17, 30, 36, 38, 106
Monida Pass 7
Montana & Southeastern 49
Montana Central 9-3, 15-19, 86, 91, 101-2, 104
Montana Free Coinage Association 91
Montana Improvement Co. 18
Montana Rail Link 41, 49-50, 54, 96
Montana Union 8, 10-13, 16, 21, 23, 28-9, 34-5, 86, 88-9, 93, 96, 100-1, 104
Montana Union Transfer 26, 28, 32, 34
Montana Western 89, 96
Morris, mayor 37
Morrison Dan 42-3
Morrison Cave 31, 42-3
Mosier, Bill 46
Mullan Pass 8-10
Mullan Tunnel 8, 13, 29, 61, 93-4
Murphy, detective 83
Murray, Mr. 91

Nielson, "Dad" 60
Nixon, R.V. 39, 47, 67, 73, 75, 95
Noble, Robert 45
Noll, G.B. 90
Norris 10, 17, 24, 31, 41, 97-8, 100-1, 103-4
North Coast Hiawatha 93, 96
North Coast Limited 29-30, 42, 36, 59, 60-1, 67, 80, 82, 88, 93-5
Northern Pacific & Montana 10, 12, 18-20, 22, 24-5, 40, 72-3, 91-2, 97-106
Northern Pacific Transport Co. 93
Norwegian Gulch 24, 41

Oakes, Thomas 14, 16, 27, 106
O'Brien, Nick 23
O'Cleary, Tom 19
Ogdan, UT 7
Oliver, conductor 89
O'Mara, John 82
Omsun's Spur 32, 52, 54
O'Reagan, William 79
Oregon Railroad & Navigation Co. 16
Oregon Short Line 10, 85
Ott, trainmaster 83

Packard, Dr. 47
Packard, Mrs. Fan 50
Palmer, fireman 90
Parker, C.C. 46
Parrot Copper & Silver Mining Co. 10, 46-7, 49, 100-1, 104
Parrot Quarry Spur 54, 62
Patterson, J.C. 22-5, 27, 29, 41, 71-3
Payne, O.H. 106
Pennycook, foreman 24
Philosophy River 39
Phoenix Electric Company 64
Piedmont 47
Pipestone 21, 24, 29, 32
Pipestone Hot Springs Hotel 50
Pipestone Pass 8, 14, 47, 49, 73, 88
Pipestone Quarry 96
Pipestone Rock 22, 33, 52, 57, 59, 64, 66

The moon rises over mile post 49 on the Butte Short Line as we look out over the Jefferson Valley near Spire Rock siding.